Tools for Learning

Activities for Young Children with Special Needs

Joanne Stafferton McElderry
Denver Public Schools

Linda Ecklund Escobedo
Denver Public Schools

LOVE PUBLISHING COMPANY
Denver · London

INSTRUCTIONAL TEACHING AIDS SERIES

Illustrations by Janus Gay

Copyright © 1979 Love Publishing Company
Printed in the U.S.A.
ISBN 0-89108-066-X
Library of Congress Catalog Card Number 76-62664
10 9 8 7 6 5 4 3 2

CONTENTS

CONTENTS

Introduction

Tools for Learning was born out of frustration with the learning problems of young handicapped children. First, specific skill areas were identified as targets. Then intrinsically motivating materials were selected. Starting with these two elements — children's specific learning needs and motivating materials — learning opportunities were structured based on sound learning principles, ways in which children learn most efficiently. Our initial efforts were reinforced by teachers and children sharing the excitement of learning in new ways. It became apparent that activities developed to meet the learning needs of specific children could also be helpful to other teachers in a variety of settings. We feel these activities are appropriate for use by:

- regular classroom teachers attempting to meet needs of handicapped children mainstreamed in the regular classroom
- teachers of children in special programs
- teachers in preschool or kindergarten programs
- teachers in Head Start or day care centers
- parents at home
- paraprofessionals or volunteers in any of the above settings.

The activities in this book are designed to emphasize *tool skills* — necessary prerequisites to academic success. Many children seem to learn these basic skills almost automatically. However, some children need structured learning opportunities which do not leave this learning to chance. Each activity in this book includes a task analysis of the tool skills which may be emphasized. This enables teachers to select activities according to the learning needs of their children. In addition, suggestions are provided for activity modification to further adjust teaching strategies to meet individual needs.

Tools for Learning attempts to demonstrate a variety of new materials and techniques to make the learning of basic skills fun for both teachers and children. We hope this material will inspire new avenues for the creativity that has always been the trademark of a good teacher. The activities are written in detail — not to supersede this creativity, but to model forms within which it may be successful!

Introductory material features a handy cross-reference of **Tool Skills,** condensed into major categories, and the activities in which they are included. Because of the heavy emphasis on development of basic language concepts, a separate concept reference is provided.

Each major section of the book is introduced with general information about securing and preparing the material which is basic to that section. The focus is on inexpensive, readily available materials which have high motivational value for young children. The reality of material preparation dictated an emphasis on multiple use of materials. The effort expended collecting and preparing sets of materials is far more rewarding if they can be used to meet a variety of teaching objectives.

Each activity in the book is organized with major headings to assist the teacher. The headings are Focus On, Materials, Group Instruction, Individual Instruction, Independent Learning Center and Meeting Individual Needs.

Introduction

FOCUS ON provides a task analysis of specific tool skills to be taught. Basic language concepts are listed.

MATERIALS begins with a list of specific materials required by the activity. When necessary, detailed instructions are included for preparation of materials. These instructions are particularly helpful if some material preparation can be delegated. Consider, for example, organizing a parent workshop to make materials. For the child who requires much practice, fresh material can take the drudgery out of skill development.

GROUP INSTRUCTION provides a step-by-step guide to the use of activities appropriate for a group lesson. The activities in this book were developed for use with groups of up to eight children. Some of the activities could easily be adapted for use with larger groups. Often group games are followed by independent learning center activities which reinforce the group learning experience.

INDIVIDUAL INSTRUCTION is required for certain activities. Instructions are specific and complete so that they may be used by aides, volunteers, parents, or older children serving as cross-age tutors.

INDEPENDENT LEARNING CENTER describes the use of materials by a child at a center, usually with a specific task structured for him. Exploration and discovery at learning centers is to be encouraged. However, children with special learning needs often require structured activity if specific learning objectives are to be achieved. Naming and describing materials, and demonstrating the sequence of a task, can often be done with a group prior to independent learning time.

MEETING INDIVIDUAL NEEDS suggests strategies for increasing the learning of children through modification of the task or the instructional approach. It is hoped that the focus will always remain on the needs of the child — picking him up wherever he may be on a developmental continuum, then guiding him to take the next step through successful learning experiences.

Appendix material is provided as a resource to teachers. Appendix A is intended to simplify material preparation for selected activities. These resources may be reproduced for teacher use. Appendix B contains instructions for preparation of materials used in more than one section. Appendix C is a source page for the purchase of materials. Appendix D is an index to facilitate location of specific information.

TOOL SKILLS CROSS-REFERENCE CHART

		Page Number	Developing Fine Motor Skills	Matching	Sequencing	Remembering	Recognizing Relationships	Using Left to Right Progression	Developing Number Concepts	Developing Basic Language Concepts	Communicating With Language
KEYS	Exploring with Keys	12	LC								
	Keys, Keys and More Keys	13	I LC	I LC				I LC		I LC	
	1, 2, 3 Key	14	I		I			I		I	I
	Peek-a-Boo Keys	17	I		I	I		I	I	I	I
	Unlock is the Key Word	20	G LC							G LC	
	Dozens of Keys	21					LC			LC	
	Lock Up!	22	LC				LC			LC	
MITTENS AND GLOVES	Thumbs Tell	24	LC	G LC			LC		G	G LC	
	Spin and Pair	28	LC	G LC		G				G LC	
	How Many Ways?	30					G		G	G	G
	Mystery Hand	32		G		G				G	G
POCKETS	Feel a Pocket	36	G							G	G
	Penny Pockets	38			LC		LC		LC	LC	
	Plentiful Pockets	40	G							G	G
	Pocket Puzzles	42				G	G			G	G
	Pocket Mystery	44	G				G			G	G
MARSH-MALLOWS	Marshmallow Cones	48			G	G	G			G	G
	Double Dip	50			G	G	G			G	

G = *Group Instruction*
I = *Individual Instruction*
LC = *Learning Center*

	Activity	Page Number	Developing Fine Motor Skills	Matching	Sequencing	Remembering	Recognizing Relationships	Using Left to Right Progression	Developing Number Concepts	Developing Basic Language Concepts	Communicating With Language
MARSH-MALLOWS	Marshmallow Lane	52	G LC			G			G LC	G LC	
	Marshmallow Equality	54	LC				LC		LC	LC	
PLASTIC EGGS	Small, Medium, and Large	58	LC	LC			LC			LC	
	Scrambled Eggs	60	G LC		G LC						
	Egg Puzzles	63	G							G	G
	Egg Hunt Surprise	66		G		G				G	G
	In An Eggshell	68		G		G		G	G	G	G
MINIATURE CLOTHING	Laundry Mix-Up	72	G LC		G LC					G LC	G
	Laundromat	74	LC				LC			LC	
	Design for Decision	76					G LC			G LC	G
	What Are You Wearing?	78	G LC				G LC			G LC	G
	Counting Clothes	80	LC				LC		LC	LC	LC
	Rainbow Laundry	82	LC	LC						LC	
SMALL BOXES	Get It Together	84	LC	LC	LC					LC	
	If The Top Fits	86	LC				LC		LC	LC	
	Deep or Shallow?	87	G			G	G	G		G	
	Penny Wise	90	G LC	G LC		G LC	G LC		G LC	G LC	G
	Don't Take It Light-ly	94	G							G	G

G = Group Instruction
I = Individual Instruction
LC = Learning Center

		Page Number	Developing Fine Motor Skills	Matching	Sequencing	Remembering	Recognizing Relationships	Using Left to Right Progression	Developing Number Concepts	Developing Basic Language Concepts	Communicating With Language
SMALL BOXES	What's Inside?	96	G	G		G				G	
	Flip Your Lid	98	G LC				G LC			G LC	G
FILM CANS	Shake a Match	103		LC				LC		LC	
	Spin and Match	105		G	G				G		G
	Do You Remember?	108		G	G					G	
	Smell a Match	110		LC				LC		LC	
	Smelly Things	112					LC			LC	
	Banana, Apple, or Nuts?	113					LC			LC	
	Smell and Think Lotto	114					G LC				G
	Which Weigh?	116	LC							LC	
HATS	Hat Shop	118					G I LC		G I LC	G I LC	G I LC
	Look at Me	122					G LC			G LC	
	Ellie and Elmer Emptyhead	124								G	G
	Ellie and Elmer at Work	128					G				G

G = *Group Instruction*
I = *Individual Instruction*
LC = *Learning Center*

THUMBTACKS

	Page Number	Developing Fine Motor Skills	Matching	Sequencing	Remembering	Recognizing Relationships	Using Left to Right Progression	Developing Number Concepts	Developing Basic Language Concepts	Communicating With Language
Tack-It #1	132	G I LC					G I LC		G I LC	
Tack-It #2	133	G I LC					G I LC		G I LC	
Tack-It #3	133	G I LC					G I LC		G I LC	
Tack-It #4	134	G I LC					G I LC		G I LC	
Tack-It #5	134	G I LC							G I LC	
Tack-It #6	135	G I LC							G I LC	
Tack-It #7	135	G I LC						G I LC	G I LC	G I LC
Tack-It #8	136	G I LC							G I LC	
Tack-It #9	136	G I LC			G I LC			G I LC	G I LC	
Tack-It #10	137	G I LC						G I LC	G I LC	
Tack-It #11	137	G I LC								
Tack-It #12	138	G I LC						G I LC	G I LC	
Tack-It #13	138	G I LC							G I LC	
Tack-It #14	138	G I LC							G I LC	
Tack-It #15	139	G I LC							G I LC	
Tack-It #16	139	G I LC							G I LC	
Tack-It #17	139	G I							G I	
Tacky Patterns	140	I		I	I		I		I	I

G = Group Instruction
I = Individual Instruction
LC = Learning Center

BASIC LANGUAGE CONCEPTS

This section is designed to provide a reference to the tool skill area "developing basic language concepts." Each specific concept is listed separately with page numbers for the activities in which it appears.

This collection of activities places heavy emphasis on the development of basic language concepts because they are fundamental as tools for learning. Teachers can often add concept learning to a lesson without adding time or energy — a kind of *bonus for children* which can make a world of difference. The critical factor is teacher awareness of concept development as a vital part of lesson planning. It is not suggested that all concepts listed with a specific activity be included in any one lesson plan. While this may be desirable with some activities, it is usually more effective to carefully select concepts for emphasis during each lesson. Those concepts selected from lesson to lesson should vary as indicated by the individual needs of the children. Presenting the same concept in several different situations and with a variety of materials may help those children who have difficulty generalizing this concept. Try adding the dimension of basic concept development to your lesson plans — you'll like the results!

The following list of basic language concepts is based on research done by Ann Boehm in development of the Boehm Test of Basic Concepts published in 1969 (The Psychological Corporation, 757 Third Avenue, New York, New York 10017). This research identified "basic concepts" as those concepts which are
- frequently used in preschool and primary-grade curriculum materials
- relatively abstract
- seldom adequately defined.

In addition to concepts from the Boehm Test of Basic Concepts, the following list includes many of the concepts excluded from the test. Based on experimental tryout of test items, a number of concepts were excluded because most children entering kindergarten already know them. If certain basic concepts are generally familiar to children beginning school, the child who does not understand these concepts will be in trouble! Since these are the very concepts that should have top priority for children with special learning needs, these concepts are included in the following list.

BASIC CONCEPTS	PAGE NUMBERS
above	13, 17, 68, 87, 137, 138
after	44, 124
alike	13, 17, 21, 32, 48, 50, 68, 96, 105, 108, 140
always	44, 124
around	44, 82, 118, 134
back	118
before	38, 44
begin	13, 14, 17, 68, 87, 132, 133, 134, 139, 140

below	13, 17, 52, 68, 78, 137, 138
beside	32, 44, 50
between	44, 132, 133
big	14, 21, 30, 32, 84, 118, 136
bottom	13, 17, 24, 42, 48, 50, 52, 68, 78, 84, 86, 98, 103, 110, 112, 116, 133, 140
center	136, 139
closed	20, 24, 32, 60, 68, 86, 87, 90, 96, 98
corner	135
curved	134
dark	30, 32, 74, 94, 118
deep	87
different	13, 17, 21, 28, 32, 48, 50, 68, 76, 78, 82, 90, 94, 96, 98, 103, 105, 108, 110, 140
down	50, 66
early	124
empty	14, 48, 87, 90, 124
equal	54, 90
every	84, 135, 136, 137, 138, 139
few	30, 40, 84, 118
finish	139
first	14, 17, 48, 50, 72, 139, 140
flat	44
follow	87
front	22, 90, 118
full	87
half	58, 60, 63, 68
hard	36, 44

Basic Concepts	Page Numbers
heavy	87, 90, 94, 116
in order	38, 72, 90
inside	20, 32, 36, 38, 40, 42, 44, 60, 63, 66, 68, 84, 86, 87, 90, 96, 98, 124, 134, 135
join	44
large	14, 21, 30, 32, 58, 60, 63, 66, 68, 84, 118, 136
last	13, 17, 48, 50, 72, 122, 139, 140
late	124
least	38, 90, 118, 135
left	13, 14, 17, 24, 30, 32, 68, 103, 110, 132, 133, 134, 139, 140
light (color)	30, 32, 74, 94, 118
light (weight)	87, 90, 94, 116
line	52, 132, 133, 134, 136, 140
little	14, 21, 30, 32, 84, 118, 136
long	80, 138
many	30, 40, 118
match	13, 17, 28, 32, 50, 52, 58, 68, 96, 98, 103, 105, 108, 110, 112, 113, 116, 138
medium-sized	30, 32, 58, 60, 63, 68, 84, 118, 136
middle	22, 48, 50, 133, 139
most	38, 90, 118, 135
narrow	118, 139
never	44, 52, 54, 124
next	13, 14, 17, 36, 40, 44, 48, 50, 68, 72, 118, 122, 140
none	122
open	20, 66, 68, 86, 87, 90, 96, 98
other	24, 28, 32, 60, 74
outside	98, 134, 135

Key Activities

MATERIALS IN COMMON

- assorted keys
- keyboard

FINDING MATERIALS

- Obtain colored keys in a variety of sizes and shapes from the many places that make duplicate keys. Miscut keys usually are available free or at nominal cost.
- Ask parents to donate old keys no longer useful around the home.

    Suggested assortment of keys:

        6 each of five colors, or 8 each of four colors
        10 silver or brass household keys in different sizes
        additional keys as available (optional)

MAKING MATERIALS

    To make the keyboard:

    1. Cut a wood board to approximately 8″ by 24″.
    2. Space cup hooks across this board in two rows, 15 hooks per row.
    3. Make a stand by nailing wood triangles to the back of the board.

HELPFUL HINT

- Draw a green arrow on masking tape and place it on the upper left corner of the keyboard to indicate starting point and direction. "The green arrow tells you where to start." Remove the masking tape arrow when a directional cue is no longer needed.

Exploring With Keys

FOCUS ON

- developing manipulative skills

MATERIALS

- assorted keys
- keyboard

INDEPENDENT LEARNING CENTER

Set up the keyboard with assorted keys at a learning center. Allow the child to put keys on and off the hooks on the keyboard in any way he chooses.

Note: Keys have a special kind of fascination for children. The keyboard with keys makes a popular manipulative toy in its own right. For this reason, it is important to provide an opportunity for free exploration with the materials *before* presenting the structured key activities.

MEETING INDIVIDUAL NEEDS

- Observe each child in order to evaluate his performance of the fine motor task involved in hanging the keys on the cup hooks. If a child has difficulty, have him practice hanging objects with larger holes. Provide objects such as curtain rings, plastic finger rings, paper clips or pop-top rings for the child to hang on the cup hooks.
- For the child who needs bilateral activities, have him remove the keys from the keyboard using both hands simultaneously.

Keys, Keys, and More Keys

FOCUS ON

- developing manipulative skills
- recognizing colors
- matching objects
- using left-to-right progression
- developing basic language concepts:
    *top, bottom, begin, left, right, above, below,
    same, different, alike, match, row, next, last*

MATERIALS

- keyboard
- 2 identical sets of colored keys, 15 keys per set

INDIVIDUAL INSTRUCTION

For an activity emphasizing basic concept development, teacher direction and descriptive language are necessary.

1. Beginning at the left, hang one set of keys across the top row of the keyboard in random order.
2. Direct the child to work from left to right across the bottom row with an identical set of keys. Have him match each key to the key directly above.
3. Talk about the child's choices as he works, choosing specific concepts to be emphasized.

INDEPENDENT LEARNING CENTER

For an independent activity emphasizing visual match, set up the keyboard at a learning center with one set of keys across the top row. Have the child:

1. Begin at the left.
2. Work across the bottom row of the keyboard with an identical set of keys, matching each key to the key directly above.

MEETING INDIVIDUAL NEEDS

- If a child needs help with color recognition, have him hang the top row of keys. "Find a red key and hang it here. Put a blue key next. Put a green key next".
- To increase the difficulty of this activity, use two identical sets of keys which are the same color. Vary the keys within a set by shape and size. Have the child match the keys without color cues.
- For the child ready for a still more challenging task, direct him to match keys on the basis of shape alone with color as a distractor — for example, a green key with a square top is paired with a blue key with the same square top.

1, 2, 3 Key

FOCUS ON

- recognizing and naming colors
- developing manipulative skills
- using left-to-right progression
- continuing sequential patterns seen
- developing basic language concepts:
    row, next, begin, big, little, large, small, skip,
    empty, left, right, first, second, third

MATERIALS

- keyboard
- colored keys

INDIVIDUAL INSTRUCTION

Arrange keys sequentially, beginning a pattern which the child continues across a row on the keyboard.

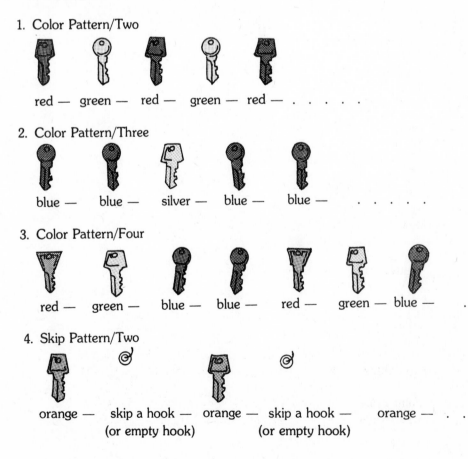

1. Color Pattern/Two

red — green — red — green — red — . . . . . .

2. Color Pattern/Three

blue — blue — silver — blue — blue — . . . . .

3. Color Pattern/Four

red — green — blue — blue — red — green — blue — . . .

4. Skip Pattern/Two

orange — skip a hook — orange — skip a hook — orange — . .
(or empty hook)   (or empty hook)

1, 2, 3 Key

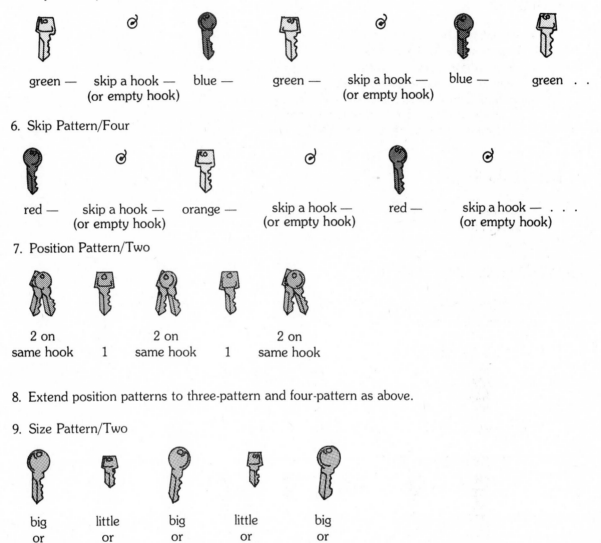

5. Skip Pattern/Three

green —   skip a hook —   blue —   green —   skip a hook —   blue —   green . .
      (or empty hook)   (or empty hook)

6. Skip Pattern/Four

red —   skip a hook —   orange —   skip a hook —   red —   skip a hook — . . .
     (or empty hook)   (or empty hook)   (or empty hook)

7. Position Pattern/Two

2 on   2 on   2 on
same hook   1   same hook   1   same hook

8. Extend position patterns to three-pattern and four-pattern as above.

9. Size Pattern/Two

big   little   big   little   big
or   or   or   or   or
large   small   large   small   large

10. Extend Size Pattern to three-pattern and four-pattern as above.

MEETING INDIVIDUAL NEEDS

- To vary the difficulty of the task, lengthen or shorten the sequence. For example, if a child is unable to continue a three-pattern, go back to many activities using a two-pattern.
- If a child has difficulty moving from one sequence level to another, have him verbalize the pattern with you until he can verbalize the next step in the sequence alone.

1, 2, 3 Key

- When verbalizing the pattern, use your voice as a cue to group the patterns for the child. For example, "Red, green, (pause), red, green, (pause), red . . . ."
- Vary the language used in presenting these tasks according to the child's level of concept development. Any of the concepts listed under "developing basic language concepts" may be emphasized — for example, ordinal number concepts (first, second, third) may be reinforced.

Peek-A-Boo Keys

FOCUS ON

- developing manipulative skills
- recognizing and naming colors
- using left to right progression
- remembering — in sequence — things seen
- remembering — in sequence — things heard
- recognizing proper names
- sequencing letters
- sequencing numerals
- developing basic language concepts:
    same, different, alike, match, begin, row,
    left, right, top, bottom, next, last, first,
    second, third, above, below

MATERIALS

- keyboard
- 2 identical sets of assorted colored keys
- piece of cloth, approximately 20″ by 30″

INDIVIDUAL INSTRUCTION

Peek-A-Boo Keys, Game I (Remembering — in Sequence — Things Seen)
1. Beginning at the left, use one set of keys to arrange a pattern on the top row of the keyboard.
2. Allow the child time to look carefully at the pattern.
3. Cover the pattern with a cloth.

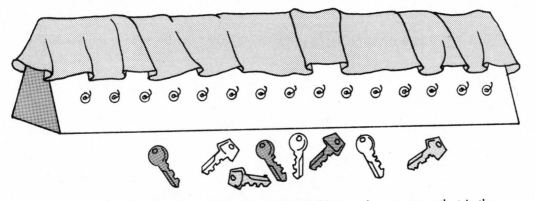

4. Using the second set of keys, ask the child to make a pattern that is the *same* on the bottom row of the keyboard.
5. Have the child lift the cloth to check his pattern. If he has made errors, encourage him to use the model on the top row to correct his pattern. (Each key must match the key directly above.) This allows every child to finish with a correct response!

Peek-A-Boo Keys

Peek-A-Boo Keys, Game II (Remembering — in Sequence — Things Heard)

1. Turn the keyboard so the child *cannot see the hooks.*
2. Use one set of keys to arrange a pattern on the top row, verbalizing the pattern as you work. "I'll *tell* you what my row looks like. Listen carefully! Red, green, red, green."
3. Cover the pattern with a cloth.
4. Turn the board to face the child.
5. Ask the child to use the second set of keys to make a pattern that is the *same* on the bottom row of the keyboard.
6. Have the child lift the cloth to check his pattern. If he has made errors, encourage him to use the model on the top row to correct his pattern. This allows each child to finish with a correct response!

Peek-A-Boo Keys, Game III (Recognizing Proper Names)

1. Use self-stick labels or masking tape to put one letter on each key, making two identical sets of lettered keys.
2. Follow instructions for Game I, spelling the name of the child.
3. Continue the game by spelling the names of other children in the class.

Some children may be able to play this game using the instructions for Game II, but knowledge of letter names is a necessary prerequisite skill.

MEETING INDIVIDUAL NEEDS

- Vary the language used in presenting these tasks according to the child's level of concept development. Emphasize any of the concepts listed under "developing basic language concepts."
- Let the child's ability level determine whether to begin with 2, 3 or 4 keys in the Game I or Game II patterns. Increase the number of keys used as the child develops skill.

Peek-A-Boo Keys

- Control the difficulty level of the task by increasing or decreasing the number of extra keys included in the child's set. Keys, in addition to those necessary to complete the pattern, serve as distractors making the task more challenging.
- A child may reproduce a pattern using the correct keys in the wrong order and not recognize this as an error when using the model to check his work. Since the emphasis is on memory for specific order, remember to point out the correct order after praising the child for his response. "Let's look at the key I have on my first hook. Is it the same as the key on your first hook?" Continue through the pattern, and then ask the child to make his row the *same* as the top row.
- To help a child who is unsuccessful, ask him to verbally repeat the sequence immediately after he sees or hears it. Then proceed with the activity.
- When playing Game II (Remembering — in Sequence — Things Heard), be aware that distraction between verbalization of the pattern and the child's opportunity to reproduce the pattern affects the difficulty of the task. To reduce difficulty level, move quickly and say nothing. To increase difficulty level, introduce distractors such as increased time lapse, conversation, background noise.
- Use Game III (Recognizing Proper Names) to prevent the practice of reversals common to many children when first learning to write their names, since lettered keys can be oriented only in one direction on the keyboard.
- To help a child who has difficulty with Game III (Recognizing Proper Names), use BACKWARD CHAINING — a procedure particularly helpful when a child's given name has several letters. It is appropriate for use with a variety of tasks. It builds in practice of each part of a task just learned, introduces only one new part of a task at a time, and allows the child to experience the satisfaction of task completion after each step.

  1. Ask the child to watch carefully as one set of keys is arranged on the top row of the keyboard to spell the child's name.
  2. Cover the name with a cloth.
  3. Arrange the second set of lettered keys on the bottom row of the keyboard, omitting the last letter of the child's name.
  4. Ask the child to hang the last key and look carefully at the completed name.
  5. Remove all the keys from the bottom row.
  6. Again hang keys to spell the child's name, this time omitting the last two letters.
  7. Ask the child to complete his name, lift the cloth to check, then make corrections if necessary.
  8. Continue this procedure, omitting one more letter each time.
  9. Finish by asking the child to hang all keys on the bottom row to spell his name!

- For practice of remembering letters and numerals in sequence, play Games I and II with letters and/or numerals attached to keys as in Game III.

Unlock is the Key Word

FOCUS ON

- developing manipulative skills
- making judgments
- developing basic language concepts:
  inside, open, closed

MATERIALS

- suitcase
- keys in assorted sizes and shapes
  including suitcase key
- colorful hats

GROUP INSTRUCTION

1. Lock a variety of hats in the suitcase.
2. Seat children in a circle, and place the suitcase and pile of keys in the center.

To play **Unlock Is the Key Word,** have each child in turn:

1. Look carefully at the suitcase lock and decide which key will open it.
2. Try to open the lock with this key.
3. If the lock will not open, hold this key until the end of the game.
4. If the lock opens, select one of the hats to wear.
5. Close and lock the suitcase.
6. Return the key to the pile of keys and mix the pile.

Continue this procedure until each child has opened the suitcase and selected a hat. Conclude with a hat parade!

INDEPENDENT LEARNING CENTER

After the group game, place the suitcase with a new surprise inside at a learning center. Use your imagination! A mask with a hand mirror is fun! Provide several keys. Trying keys to unlock the surprise becomes a motivational activity to develop fine motor coordination for the individual child.

MEETING INDIVIDUAL NEEDS

- Since this game becomes progressively easier as keys are eliminated, begin with the most capable children.
- Control the difficulty level of each game by varying the number and similarity of keys provided.

Dozens of Keys

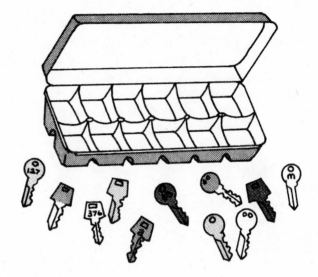

FOCUS ON

- recognizing colors
- classifying
- classifying by multiple attributes
- developing basic language concepts:
  *alike, different, with, without,
  big, little, large, small*

MATERIALS

- all available keys
- egg carton

INDEPENDENT LEARNING CENTER

1. Ask the child to put the keys into egg carton sections in groups that are *alike* in some way.
2. When the child has finished, ask him to tell you how each group of keys is *alike*.
3. Mix the keys, and ask the child to find some *different* ways to put them in groups.
4. When the child has gone as far as he is able on the basis of exploration and discovery, help him expand his classification skills by suggesting new categories, a few at a time.

> Some ways to sort keys:
> color — shape — size
> broken — not broken
> rusty — not rusty
> with numbers — without numbers
> with letters — without letters
> not cut — cut on one side — cut on both sides
> one color — more than one color
> one hole in the top — more than one hole in the top
> hole in the top that is round — hole in the top that is not round

MEETING INDIVIDUAL NEEDS

- The ability to classify is interrelated with the development of language. For children with learning problems, it is often helpful and sometimes necessary to suggest categories after initial exploration if language development is to be facilitated. Left to discovery, many of these children will not develop categorizing skills or expand their language usage.
- To make the task more challenging, suggest categories based on multiple attributes or characteristics — for example, red keys with square tops, blue keys with numbers, silver keys with more than one hole in the top.

Lock Up!

FOCUS ON

- developing manipulative skills
- relating keys to objects
- developing basic language concepts:
  middle, front

MATERIALS

- keyboard
- 10 keys
- 10 picture cards

To make picture cards:
1. Glue pictures from Appendix A-1 onto ten 3″ x 5″ cards.
2. Cover with clear contact.
3. Punch holes in the cards to fit over the cuphooks on the keyboard.

INDEPENDENT LEARNING CENTER

Set up the keyboard with the ten picture cards and an assortment of ten keys at a learning center. Challenge a child to use his thinking skills by playing **Lock Up.** Have the child:

1. Hang the pictures on the keyboard.
2. Decide which of the things pictured should have a key.
3. Hang a key on the middle hook in front of each picture of something that should have a key.

Discuss an apparent incorrect answer with the child. Accept and praise any response based on logical, reasonable associations of keys with the things pictured.

MEETING INDIVIDUAL NEEDS

- To make **Lock Up** more challenging, provide actual keys for things pictured such as a suitcase key, jewelry box key, car key, house key. Ask the child to match the appropriate key to the picture.

Mitten and Glove Activities

MATERIALS IN COMMON

- assorted mittens and gloves, both paired and unpaired

FINDING MATERIALS

Suggested sources for mittens and gloves:

- Goodwill, Salvation Army, or other used clothing stores
- rummage sales, garage sales, flea markets
- school lost-and-found boxes
- parents, relatives, neighbors, and friends (ask for unpaired, worn out, or outgrown mittens and gloves)

HELPFUL HINTS

- Select mittens and gloves with as much variety as possible. Consider:

  color   texture
  pattern or design material
  condition   function
  size   style

- If more paired mittens and gloves are needed, borrow the children's mittens and gloves for the duration of a game.

Thumbs Tell

FOCUS ON

- matching objects to pictures
- using tactile-kinesthetic information
- counting
- classifying
- classifying by multiple attributes
- developing basic language concepts:
    left, right, top, bottom, closed, other

MATERIALS

- assorted mittens and gloves, paired and/or unpaired
- mitten and glove cards
- hand markers
- organizing boxes
- blindfold (see Appendix B)
- large shallow box lid

To make mitten and glove cards:
> Trace around each mitten and each glove, with the thumbs up, on a tagboard card. Have these cards show outlines and thumb lines only, not internal detail such as design and color.

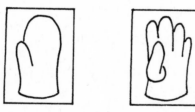

Suggestions for hand markers:

happy face sticker	piece of masking tape
coin or shape stamp	nail polish on thumb nail
ring	gummed seal
toy watch	piece of yarn around wrist

GROUP INSTRUCTION

1. Seat children around assorted mittens and gloves.
2. Place the mitten and glove cards in a pile, face down.
3. Identify left and right hands.
4. Place one hand marker on each child's left hand.
5. Discuss the difference between a mitten and a glove.

Thumbs Tell

To play **Thumbs Tell,** have each child in turn:

1. Draw a card from the top of the pile.
2. Answer these questions:
   "Does the picture show a mitten or a glove?"
   "Does the mitten (glove) in the picture go on a right hand or a left hand?"
3. Find the mitten or glove pictured.
4. Check choice by placing it, thumb up, on picture.
5. Retain card if choice was correct, or return card to bottom of pile if choice was incorrect.
6. Return mitten or glove to play.

Continue until the pile of cards is gone. End with each child counting his cards.

INDEPENDENT LEARNING CENTER I

Use four of the mitten and glove cards as cue cards. Put assorted mittens and gloves at the center. Explain that the task is to sort by two attributes:

1. Is it a mitten or a glove?
2. Does it go on a right hand or a left hand?

Sorting into boxes will help the child organize his work.

Thumbs Tell

Be sure the left cue cards are on the child's left and the right cue cards are on his right. Verbalize this relationship for him before he begins the task.

INDEPENDENT LEARNING CENTER II

Provide a blindfold, assorted mittens and gloves in a large shallow box lid, and two organizing boxes. Have the child:

1. Close his eyes and put on the blindfold.
2. Sort mittens into one organizing box and gloves into the other.
3. Remove blindfold to check.

Thumbs Tell

INDEPENDENT LEARNING CENTER III

Provide a blindfold, assorted mittens and gloves in a large shallow box lid, and two organizing boxes. Have the child:

1. Close his eyes and put on the blindfold.
2. Sort mittens and gloves into right and left, putting right in the box on his right, left in the box on his left.

MEETING INDIVIDUAL NEEDS

- When playing **Thumbs Tell** as a group game, remember that some children will use size cues and configuration details for matching cards to mittens and gloves while others will attend only to matching on the basis of the two attributes:

  1. Does it go on a right hand, or a left hand?
  2. Is it a mitten or a glove?

  Accept both kinds of response, allowing each child to play the game at his own level.
- For children having difficulty with the Independent Learning Center III activity, suggest one of the following strategies:

  1. Try on the mitten (glove) to determine whether it is left or right.
  2. Lay the mitten (glove) on the table with the thumb facing up, then place the hand (palm up) on the mitten (glove) to determine whether it is left or right.

  Combine these strategies with use of masking tape as a marker on the left wrist or forearm if needed.

- To increase the difficulty of the task in Independent Learning Center I, mix the cue cards so that the cue card for the right mitten or glove is not necessarily on the child's right side.

Spin and Pair

FOCUS ON

- matching objects
- using tactile-kinesthetic information
- remembering things seen
- developing basic language concepts:
  pair, other, match, same, different

MATERIALS

- assorted pairs of mittens and gloves
- open-ended spinner (see Appendix B)
- large, shallow box lid
- blindfold (see Appendix B)

GROUP INSTRUCTION

1. Divide mittens and gloves into two piles by putting one from each pair in each pile.
2. Spread one pile beside the open-ended spinner, and place one mitten or glove in each spinner section.

3. Spread the other pile across the room in a spot where the spinner is not visible.

To play **Spin and Pair,** have each child in turn:

1. Spin the spinner.
2. Look carefully at the indicated mitten or glove.
3. Go across the room to the pile of mittens and gloves.
4. Search for the other mitten or glove to make a pair, bring it back to the spinner, and check.

Remove all paired mittens and gloves from play. Fill empty spinner sections from the pile beside the spinner.

Spin and Pair

INDEPENDENT LEARNING CENTER

Provide a blindfold and assorted pairs of mittens and gloves in a large, shallow box lid. Have the child:

1. Close his eyes and put on the blindfold.
2. Find a *pair* of mittens or gloves.
3. Put this pair on the table beside the box lid.
4. See how many pairs he can make.
5. Remove blindfold to check.

MEETING INDIVIDUAL NEEDS

- Because the difficulty level of both the group game and the independent activity depends on the similarity of the mittens and gloves and the number of pairs included, change these variables to meet the needs of the children.
- Since some children find matching on the basis of tactile-kinesthetic information alone a very difficult task, help these children by beginning the independent activity with as few as three very different pairs (rubber gloves, wool mittens, leather gloves).
- If the children are having difficulty with the concept *pair*, demonstrate the concept each time a pair is completed in the group game by having the child put on the mittens (gloves) and hold up his hands wearing a *pair*.

How Many Ways?

FOCUS ON

- recognizing and naming colors
- counting
- naming common materials
- relating part to whole
- using descriptive language
- developing basic language concepts:
  left, right, big, little, large, small, medium-sized, light, dark, several, few, many

MATERIALS

- assorted, unpaired, mittens and gloves
- game tokens

Suggestions for game tokens:

bottle caps	charms	bread tags
beans	paper clips to chain	acorns
buttons	peanuts in the shell	small stones

GROUP INSTRUCTION

1. Seat children around a pile of mittens and gloves.
2. Allow each child, in turn, to choose one mitten or glove.
3. Give the child one game token for each different way he can describe his mitten or glove.
4. Count the tokens at the end of each turn.

Encourage the children to talk about:

1. label: left mitten, right glove
2. color: light, dark, color names
3. number: one, two, several, few, many (related to color or pattern)
4. size: big, little, large, small, medium-sized
5. condition: old, new, dirty, clean
6. material: wool, leather, rubber, cotton, plastic, nylon
7. pattern or design: stripes, dots, checks, snowman, triangles
8. parts: thumb, fingers, cuff, palm, lining
9. function: warmth (to play in the snow), safety (to play baseball), protection (to scrub the floor), beauty (to wear to a wedding)

How Many Ways?

MEETING INDIVIDUAL NEEDS

- For a child who is having difficulty with the descriptive language task, provide assistance through RESPONSE STRUCTURING.* Alter teacher direction by moving down through the levels indicated below as far as necessary to secure a successful response. Reinforce this response immediately with praise. Note the response level which is comfortable for the child. This may provide information to help build response skills in other settings. Over a period of time, be aware of helping this child move to higher response levels.

Child Response Level	Teacher Direction or Question Level
RECALL	Focus on specific topic for expression. "Tell me about the glove." Ask WH question. "What color is this glove?" Ask completion question. "The color of this glove is _____?"
RECOGNITION	Ask multiple choice question. "Is this glove red or blue?" Ask question requiring yes or no. "Is this glove red?"
IMITATION	Provide complete model for response, and ask child to imitate. "This glove is red."

- Begin this game with those children who have the best verbal skills, as their verbalizations will provide a model for the other children.
- When a child gives a description that is not a sentence, model this description in a full sentence.

"thumb"	"This mitten has a thumb."
"rubber glove"	"This glove is made of rubber."

*RESPONSE STRUCTURING is a valuable technique which can be used across a variety of learning activities. Teachers are tempted to "rescue" a child who cannot respond, by moving on to a more capable child who provides the answer, (i.e. "Valerie, can you help Bill?"). In such a situation, however, the capable child who does not need practice is the one to receive it. RESPONSE STRUCTURING can provide appropriate practice for *each* child by moving to easier levels until a successful response is received.

Mystery Hand

FOCUS ON

- matching objects
- remembering things heard
- using descriptive language
- developing basic language concepts:
    *other, pair, inside, same, different, alike,
    match, left, right, big, little, large, small,
    medium-sized, light, dark, several, beside, closed*

MATERIALS

- assorted pairs of mittens and gloves
- large box open on one side

GROUP INSTRUCTION

1. Seat children around a table.
2. Spread one mitten or glove from each pair on the table.
3. Put the other mitten or glove from each pair in a large box placed with the opening away from the children.
4. Talk about the mittens and gloves, reviewing concepts and descriptive language from the preceding activity, **How Many Ways?**

To play **Mystery Hand,** have each child in turn:

1. Go to the box and choose a mitten or glove.
2. Put the mitten or glove on his hand, keeping it *inside* the box where the other children cannot see it.
4. Tell *one* thing about his mitten (glove), then choose a child, and say, "Find the other mitten (glove) to make a pair."
4. If a pair is not made, add a different description about the mitten (glove), select another child, and give the same direction to the new child selected, "Find the *other* mitten (glove) to make a pair."
5. When a pair is made, show the "mystery hand" to everyone.

Continue the game by letting the child who makes the pair choose the next mystery mitten or glove.

Mystery Hand

MEETING INDIVIDUAL NEEDS

- Since the difficulty level of the game depends on the similarity of the mittens and gloves, and the number of mitten and glove choices provided, change these variables to meet the needs of the children.
- Increase the challenge of the game by adding unpaired mittens and gloves as distractors on the table. (Do *not* put unpaired mittens and gloves in the box!)
- If a child is having difficulty with the concept *pair,* demonstrate the concept each time a pair is completed by having the child put on the other mitten (glove) and hold up his hands wearing a *pair.*
- Since no one knows who is to be chosen next in this game, emphasize that it is important for *all* children to remember each description. Some children will quickly discover this. Others will need to be reminded to "listen and remember."

Pocket
Activities

MATERIALS IN COMMON

- pocket cards
- pocket game tokens

FINDING MATERIALS

- Ask parents of students, other teachers, your own family, and friends to save discarded clothing with pockets.

MAKING MATERIALS

To make pocket cards:

1. Remove pockets from discarded clothing. Leave some of the surrounding fabric attached to the pockets — across the top only, or all the way around — depending on pocket design.
2. Staple pockets onto 7" x 11" posterboard cards. Staple only one pocket per card.

To make pocket game tokens:

1. Draw small pockets on a ditto.
2. Run the ditto on tagboard.
3. Cut pocket tokens.

HELPFUL HINTS

- To increase either quantity or variety of pocket cards, use fabric scraps and make a few new pockets.

Feel A Pocket

FOCUS ON

- using tactile-kinesthetic information
- naming common objects
- using descriptive language
- giving directions
- developing basic language concepts:
  hard, soft, inside, next

MATERIALS

- pocket cards
- hard and soft objects
- pocket game tokens

Suggestions for hard and soft objects:

hard		**soft**	
walnut	comb	washcloth	small sock
small rock	penny	cotton	soft toy
small box	large nail	sponge	small mitten
small bottle	large button	yarn	handkerchief
small scissors	key	Kleenex	powder puff

Helpful hints

- Introduce concepts such as hard and soft in activities utilizing a variety of materials to facilitate generalization by the child.
- Provide hard and soft objects that are easy for children to name.

GROUP INSTRUCTION

1. Seat the children in a circle, allow each to select a pocket card, and have each in turn:

   - Choose one object, feel it, and name it.
   - Tell whether the object is hard or soft.
   - Put the object into the pocket.

2. Mix these pocket cards and spread them in the center of the circle.
3. Choose a child, and have him:

   - "Find a pocket with something soft (hard) inside. Don't peek! *Feel* the pockets."
   - Guess which soft (hard) thing is inside the chosen pocket.
   - Check by removing contents of the pocket.

Feel A Pocket

4. Reward a correct choice with a pocket game token.
5. Have the child who just completed a turn choose the next child, and give him directions to find a pocket with something hard (soft) inside.

MEETING INDIVIDUAL NEEDS

- To increase the difficulty level of this game, have each child fill more than one pocket card to put in the center of the circle.
- To help a child who is having difficulty focusing on tactile-kinesthetic information, suggest feeling the pockets with eyes closed.

Penny Pockets

FOCUS ON

- counting
- using one-to-one correspondence
- recognizing numerals
- sequencing numerals
- relating numerals to quantity
- recognizing odd and even numbers
- developing basic language concepts:
  inside, in order, least, most, before

MATERIALS

- 10 pocket cards
- 55 pennies
- number markers

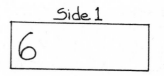

To make number markers:

1. Cut tagboard into ten 2″ by 6″ pieces.
2. Put a numeral from 1-10 on Side 1.
3. Put the same numeral and a corresponding number of penny-pictures on Side 2.
4. Attach a paper clip.

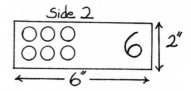

Helpful Hint:

To make penny-pictures simply draw around a penny, or use a penny stamp from a coin stamp set (see Appendix C).

INDEPENDENT LEARNING CENTER

Clip number markers, with Side 1 up, to the bottoms of ten pocket cards. Put the pocket cards and the pennies at a learning center.

Penny Pockets

Have the child:

1. Put one penny into the 1 pocket.
2. Put two pennies into the 2 pocket.
3. Continue until all pockets have the correct number of pennies inside.
4. Check the completed task:
   - Remove the number marker from a pocket card and turn it over.
   - Remove the pennies from the pocket.
   - Put the pennies on top of the penny pictures. If there is one penny for each picture of a penny, the task was completed correctly.
   - Repeat for each pocket.

MEETING INDIVIDUAL NEEDS

- Vary the selection of cards for this activity according to the needs of the children. For example:

  1. Simplify the task by beginning with cards 1-5 only.
  2. Emphasize even numbers by using cards 2, 4, 6, 8, 10 only.
  3. Emphasize odd numbers by using cards 1, 3, 5, 7, 9 only.

- For a child who is having difficulty with numeral recognition, set up the learning center with the number markers *inside* the pockets.

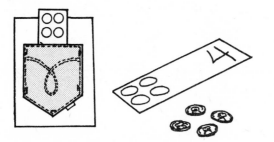

Have the child:

1. Remove a number marker from a pocket.
2. Place pennies on the picture side of the card, carefully matching one penny to one picture.
3. Put the pennies into the pocket.
4. Clip the number marker to the pocket card.
5. Continue until all pockets have pennies inside.

Help the child check by counting the pennies in each pocket.

- For a child who has mastered numerical sequence, provide sequencing practice and concept instruction by placing all ten cards at the center in a pile. Ask the child to put the cards *in order* from least to most before putting pennies into the pockets.

Plentiful Pockets

FOCUS ON

- using tactile-kinesthetic information
- naming common objects
- developing basic language concepts:
  few, many, inside, next

MATERIALS

- 8 pocket cards
- small objects
- object bag
- shallow container such as box top or tray
- pocket game tokens

To prepare pocket cards:

1. Select four kinds of small objects.
2. Put a *few* of each object in one pocket, *many* of each object in another pocket.

Suggestions for small objects:

pennies	small sea shells
dry beans	small stones
buttons	nuts in the shell
keys	acorns

To prepare object bag:

Put into a bag one example of each kind of small object selected.

Helpful hints

- Introduce concepts such as few and many in activities utilizing a *variety* of objects to facilitate generalization by the child.
- Vary the number of objects used to illustrate few, and the number of objects used to illustrate many, so that children will not associate these concepts with a specific number. For example:

few	**many**
3 pennies	18 pennies
5 dry beans	40 dry beans
4 keys	12 keys

Plentiful Pockets

GROUP INSTRUCTION

1. Seat the children in a circle.
2. Remove the objects from the object bag, and help the children name them.
3. Use two pockets, each containing the same object, to demonstrate the concepts *few* and *many*:

   > "Some pockets have a *few* things in them." (Empty "few" pocket into shallow container; return objects to pocket.)
   >
   > "Some pockets have *many* things in them." (Empty as above.)

4. Continue to demonstrate in this way, asking the children to help identify *few* and *many*, until all pockets have been discussed.
5. Mix the pocket cards, and spread them in the center of the circle.
6. Have each child in turn:

   - Draw one object from the object bag and name it.
   - Search for a pocket containing objects like the one drawn. Children may *feel* the pockets, but must not peek.
   - Select one pocket and answer, "Does it have a *few* or many _____ inside?"
   - Empty the pocket into the container to check.
   - Choose the next child to have a turn.

7. Reward correct responses with a pocket game token.
8. Return objects to pocket, and return pocket to play.

Pocket Puzzles

FOCUS ON

- naming common objects
- relating objects to pockets
- remembering relationships
- remembering things seen and heard
- developing basic language concepts:
    inside, top, bottom

MATERIALS

- pocket cards
- assorted objects
- pocket puzzle cue cards (*see* Appendix A-2)
- pocket game tokens

To prepare pocket cards:

Put these objects	**inside these pockets**
1. small screw driver	blue jeans pocket
2. small address book	shirt pocket
3. comb	jacket pocket
4. billfold	pants pocket
5. handkerchief	dress pocket
6. rubber glove	apron pocket
7. nickel and penny	billfold pocket
8. key	purse pocket
9. curler	robe pocket
10. plastic rain hat	raincoat pocket
11. mitten	heavy coat pocket
12. Band-Aid	nurse's uniform pocket
13. three marbles	child's jeans pocket
14. miniature doll	child's dress pocket
15. balloon	child's jacket pocket

GROUP INSTRUCTION

1. Display pocket cards in full view of all the children.
2. Identify each pocket as you put an object into it. For example, "This white pocket was on a nurse's uniform. I am putting a Band-Aid inside the nurse's pocket."
3. As you put objects into pockets, remind the children to remember what is inside each pocket. "The kind of pocket will help you remember what I put inside."
4. Place cue cards in a pile, face down.

Pocket Puzzles

To play **Pocket Puzzles,** have each child in turn:

1. Take one cue card from the top of the pile.
2. Try to remember which pocket contains the object pictured on the cue card.
3. Select this pocket, and remove its contents to check.
4. Return the pocket to its place, and put the cue card on the *bottom* of the pile.
5. Receive a pocket game token for a correct choice.

MEETING INDIVIDUAL NEEDS

• Adapt the difficulty level of this game to the needs of a specific group by adjusting the number of pocket cards used. Begin with as few as three cards. Increase the **number of pocket cards** as children become successful.

Pocket Mystery

FOCUS ON

- using tactile-kinesthetic information
- naming common objects
- relating two objects
- relating objects to functions
- developing basic language concepts:
  inside, next, through, round, flat, around, separate, always, pair, before, after, hard, soft, join, between, beside, never

Something made of soft rubber for a baby to drink through

MATERIALS

- pocket cards
- mystery objects
- riddle cards

Suggestions for pocket mysteries:

Mystery object to go deep inside pocket	Riddle to write on card and slip half way into pocket
thread (on a spool)	"Something that goes *through* a needle"
buckle	"Something that a belt goes *through*"
comb	"Something your hair goes *through* to make it look nice"
nipple	"Something made of soft rubber for a baby to drink *through*"
key ring	"Something that is *round* and goes *through* a key"
short plastic straw	"Something to drink *through* that is made of plastic"
two-hole button	"Something *round* and *flat* with two holes for thread to go *through*"
ball	"Something that is *round* and can bounce"
balloon	"Something that gets bigger when you put air *inside*"
sock	"Something a foot goes *inside*"
mitten/glove	"Something a hand goes *inside*"
bracelet	"Something to wear *around* the wrist"
necklace	"Something to wear *around* the neck"
large rubber band	"Something to put *around* things you don't want *separated*"
curler	"Something hair goes *around*"
ring	"Something to wear *around* a finger"
mitten/sock/earring	"Something to wear and you *always* need a *pair*"
coin	"Something you *always* need *before* using a pay telephone"

Pocket Mystery

can opener	"Something *always* needed *before* removing food from a can"
car key	"Something a driver *always* needs to start a car"
clothespin	"Something to use *after* washing clothes"
bone	"Something left *after* dinner that a dog would like"
eraser	"Something to use *after* you make a mistake with a pencil"
marshmallow	"Something that is *soft* when you buy it, but gets *hard after* it is removed from the package"
large birthday candle	"Something to light *before* you eat a birthday cake"
large nail	"Something that is hammered to *join* pieces of wood"
roll of Scotch tape or bottle of glue	"Something that can *join* two pieces of paper"
toothpick	"Something made of wood that is used to clean *between* teeth"
spoon	"Something that goes *beside* a knife to set the table"
package of gum	"Something you chew but *never* swallow"

GROUP INSTRUCTION

Choose 10 to 15 pocket mysteries according to the basic concepts to be emphasized. Seat children in a circle.

To play **Pocket Mystery**, Game I:

1. Spread pocket mysteries in the center of the circle.
2. Remove the riddle card from one pocket saying, "Inside this pocket is . . . (read the riddle card)."
3. Ask one child at a time, "What do you think is inside the pocket? You may feel the pocket, but don't peek!"
4. When a child can name an object he thinks is inside the pocket, have him remove the object to check.
5. If he is correct, let him choose the mystery pocket for the next child.
6. If he is incorrect, and if no one else can name the object, show it to all the children and supply the correct name.
7. Remove each pocket from play when the mystery object has been named. Keep two piles:

   - A pile for mysteries children solved
   - A pile for mysteries with solutions which had to be supplied

8. When all the pocket mysteries are gone from the center of the circle, begin again using only the pile the children could not solve.
9. Begin a third time if there are still mysteries the children could not solve.
10. Continue to Game II immediately, or begin a later lesson with Game II.

Pocket Mystery

To play **Pocket Mystery,** Game II:

1. Remove the riddle cards as you place pocket mysteries in the center of the circle.
2. Ask one child to choose a riddle card.
3. Read the riddle.
4. Ask the child to search for the pocket with the mystery object. He may feel the pockets, but must not peek!
5. Ask the child to name the object he thinks is inside the pocket before removing it to check.
6. If choice was correct:

    - Remove pocket from play.
    - Ask another child to choose a riddle card.

    If choice was incorrect:
    - Put the object back inside the pocket.
    - Read the same riddle card again, and let another child search for the mystery object.

7. Continue until no pockets remain.

MEETING INDIVIDUAL NEEDS

- Since Game II becomes easier as the number of choices decreases, begin this game with the most capable children.
- Praise all logical ideas. If Game II does not immediately follow Game I, a child may search for an object which is a logical answer to the riddle but different from the object provided. For example, the riddle may read, "Something that is soft when you buy it, but gets hard after it is removed from the package." Rather than look for a marshmallow, a child might search for a slice of bread. Talk about what a child is trying to find and, again, praise all logical ideas!

Marshmallow Activities

MATERIALS IN COMMON

- marshmallows
- ice cream cone cards
- miniature marshmallows

MAKING MATERIALS

To prepare large marshmallows for use as a permanent teaching material:

1. Cut marshmallow-sized circles of colored construction paper.
2. Glue one circle on the top of each marshmallow.
3. Place marshmallows on a cookie sheet, being careful that the sides do not touch.
4. Include marshmallows without construction paper circles for activities requiring white.
5. Place a second cookie sheet on top of the marshmallows.
6. Put two heavy books on top of the second cookie sheet.
7. Leave marshmallows weighted in this way for at least 24 hours.
8. Remove books and top cookie sheet and allow marshmallows to dry.

To make ice cream cone cards:

1. Cut cone shapes from brown construction paper.
2. Glue the cone shapes to half sheets of colored construction paper.
3. Cover with clear contact for permanence.

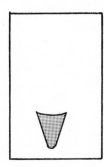 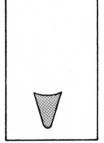

Marshmallow Cones

FOCUS ON

- recognizing and naming colors
- recognizing and naming flavors
- relating flavor names to color
- remembering — in sequence — things seen
- remembering — in sequence — things heard
- developing basic language concepts:
    *same, different, alike, empty, first, second,
    third, bottom, middle, top, next, last*

MATERIALS

- sets of dry marshmallows
- ice cream cone cards
- box lid to cover one ice cream cone card
- fresh miniature marshmallows

Sets of marshmallows contain two each of the following:

pink (strawberry)
brown (chocolate)
white (vanilla)

GROUP INSTRUCTION

1. Seat children in a line (not a circle).
2. Provide identical sets of marshmallows for each child and for the teacher.
3. Provide an ice cream cone card for each child and for the teacher.
4. Discuss the flavor name for each of the marshmallow colors.

To play **Marshmallow Cones,** Game I (Remembering — in Sequence — Things Seen):

1. Place two colored marshmallows on the teacher's cone card to provide a model cone.
2. Allow time for the children to look at the model.
3. Cover the model cone with the box lid.
4. Ask the children to make cones that are the same as the model.
5. Remove the box lid.
6. Have the children check their work and correct any errors.
7. As soon as children are ready, model three and four dip cones.

Marshmallow Cones

8. As you play the game, talk about the children's cones in terms of the basic concepts to be taught.
      "This cone is *empty*."
      "What color (flavor) did you put on your cone *first, second, third?*"
      "What color (flavor) did you put on the *bottom, middle, top?*"
      "What color (flavor) did you put *first, next, last?*"
9. End the game by giving each child a fresh miniature marshmallow to eat.

To play **Marshmallow Cones,** Game II (Remembering — in Sequence — Things Heard):

1. Place the model cone card where children cannot see it.
2. As you put two colored marshmallows on the model cone card, verbalize the pattern for the children. Choose basic concepts to be emphasized and use them consistently throughout the game. See examples above.
3. Ask children to make cones that are the same as the model.
4. Show children the model cone.
5. Have the children check their work and correct any errors.
6. As soon as children are ready, verbally model three and four dip cones.
7. End the game by giving each child a fresh miniature marshmallow to eat.

MEETING INDIVIDUAL NEEDS

- For those children who are able, begin with three dip cones.
- Use partial sets of marshmallows for children who are having difficulty. If necessary, reduce the choices to the exact number of marshmallows needed, helping the children focus attention on sequence.
- Provide the children with *both* auditory and visual information as an aid to the memory task by making sure the model is visible *and* the pattern is verbalized.
- When verbalizing patterns, use either color or flavor names. To play Game II (Remembering — in Sequence — Things Heard) using flavor names, children must associate flavor with color.
- When children are ready for a more challenging task, add colors such as green (lime), yellow (lemon), orange (orange).

Double Dip

FOCUS ON

- recognizing colors
- relating flavor names to color
- remembering — in sequence — things seen
- developing basic language concepts:
    *same, different, alike, down, beside, match, bottom,
    middle, top, next, first, second, third, last*

MATERIALS

- dry marshmallows in a bag
- ice cream cone cards
- ice cream pattern cards
- fresh miniature marshmallows

Marshmallows should be in three colors:

    pink (strawberry
    brown (chocolate)
    white (vanilla)

To make ice cream pattern cards:

1. Cut colored construction paper into half sheets.
2. Cut cone shapes from brown construction paper.
3. Cut marshmallow-sized circles from pink, brown, and white construction paper.
4. Glue cones and circles in ice cream cone patterns, with a different color pattern on each card.

Two-dip patterns   or   Three-dip patterns   or   Four-dip patterns

 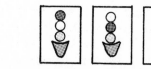 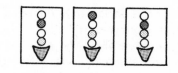

Display a different color pattern for each card.

5. Cover cards with clear contact for permanence.

GROUP INSTRUCTION

1. Give each child one ice-cream cone card.
2. Place ice-cream pattern cards in a pile, face down.
3. Discuss the flavor name for each of the marshmallow colors.

To play **Double Dip:**

1. Ask each child to take a pattern card from the top of the pile, look at it carefully, and place it face down beside his ice-cream cone card.

Double Dip

2. Explain that each child must remember this ice-cream cone and make one that is just the same. Have each child in turn:

   - Reach in the bag, and draw two marshmallows.
   - Decide whether he can use these flavors to make his cone.
   - Place those he can use on his cone.
   - Return those he cannot use to the bag.

3. Continue play until a child thinks he has an ice-cream cone that is just the same as his pattern card. Have him look at the pattern card to check.

   If ice-cream cone matches pattern card, have the child:

   - Retain the pattern card.
   - Draw a new pattern card from the top of the pile.
   - Look carefully at the new card.
   - Place the new card face down beside his cone card.
   - Remember this new pattern as he waits for his next turn.

   If ice-cream cone does not match pattern card, have the child:

   - Look carefully again at the pattern card.
   - Return the pattern card face down beside his cone card.
   - Try again to remember the pattern as play continues.

   In either case, after checking his pattern card, have the child put all his marshmallows back into the bag; play moves to the next child.

4. End the game by giving each child one fresh miniature marshmallow in exchange for each pattern card earned.

MEETING INDIVIDUAL NEEDS

- Choose a set of two dip, three dip, or four dip pattern cards based on the ability level of the group of children. Do not mix two, three, and four dip pattern cards in the same pile. If you want to play Double Dip with a group of children who are at very different levels, give each child his own pile of pattern cards with two dip for some children, three or four dip for others.
- Choose basic language concepts to be taught, and use them consistently throughout the game as you discuss the patterns:

  1. bottom, top — bottom, middle, top — bottom, next, next, top
  2. first, second — first, second, third — first, second, third, fourth
  3. first, last — first, next, last — first, next, next, last

Marshmallow Lane

FOCUS ON

- developing manipulative skills
- matching numerals
- recognizing and naming numerals
- remembering things seen and heard
- developing basic language concepts:
  bottom, match, never, line, below

MATERIALS

- numbered sets of dry marshmallows
- game board
- kitchen tongs
- fresh miniature marshmallows

To prepare numbered sets of marshmallows:

Number four sets from 1-10 by writing one numeral on the bottom of each dry marshmallow with a black marking pen. Put a line below the <u>6</u> and the <u>9</u> to avoid confusion.

To prepare game board:

1. Use 22″ x 28″ poster board.
2. Place Witch's Candy House in upper right corner (see Appendix A-3).
3. Draw and number four Marshmallow Lanes as illustrated, and cover the board with clear contact. (Circles in lanes should be slightly larger than marshmallows.)

GROUP INSTRUCTION

It is fun to read the story of Hansel and Gretel before building Marshmallow Lanes to the Witch's Candy House.

1. Seat two, three, or four children in front of the game board.
2. Put one set of marshmallows for each child on the left side of the game board, numerals down.
3. Tell the children they will play a game with the marshmallows but *they must never touch them* with their hands.
4. Provide kitchen tongs, and demonstrate picking up marshmallows with them.
5. Assign one Marshmallow Lane to each child.

Marshmallow Lane

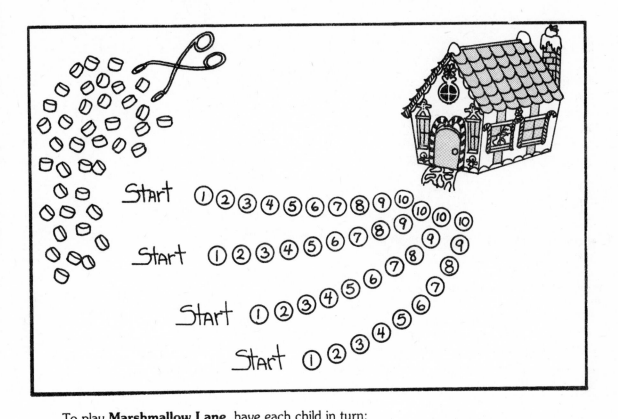

To play **Marshmallow Lane,** have each child in turn:

1. Use the tongs to lift one marshmallow, and look at the numeral on the bottom.
2. Name the numeral. (Tell the children <u>6</u> and <u>9</u> have lines below them.)
3. Place the marshmallow on the matching numeral in his lane.
4. If the matching numeral in his lane is covered, return the marshmallow to the left side of the game board, numeral down.

Give each child one fresh miniature marshmallow when his Marshmallow Lane reaches the Witch's Candy House.

INDEPENDENT LEARNING CENTER

Place the game board and one set of dry marshmallows at a learning center with the kitchen tongs. Instruct the child to use the tongs to build one Marshmallow Lane to the Witch's Candy House. Numerals must be matched. Marshmallows must *never* be touched!

MEETING INDIVIDUAL NEEDS

- Be aware that most children will initially choose marshmallows at random. Some will discover the value of remembering where numerals are returned; for others, a reminder will be helpful.

Marshmallow Equality

FOCUS ON

- developing manipulative skills
- recognizing numerals
- using one-to-one correspondence
- relating numerals to quantity
- developing basic language concepts:
  equal, never

MATERIALS

- dry marshmallows
- kitchen tongs
- equal boards (see Appendix B)
- numeral cards
- fresh miniature marshmallows

To make numeral cards:

1. Put a numeral on one side of a 4″ x 6″ card.
2. Put the corresponding number of marshmallow-sized circles on the other side of the card.

INDEPENDENT LEARNING CENTER

1. Put out a container of dry marshmallows and the kitchen tongs.
2. Select from 2 to 10 numeral cards. The number of cards and the numerals on the cards will depend on the learning needs of the child.
3. Lay out 2 to 10 equal boards; and place a numeral card, numeral side up, on one side of the = sign.
4. Tell the child, "In this game you must *never* touch the marshmallows with your hands!"
5. Have the child:

   - Use the tongs to place the indicated number of marshmallows on each equal board.
   - Check by turning over the numeral card and using one-to-one correspondence.

6. Reward task completion with a fresh miniature marshmallow.

Marshmallow Equality

MEETING INDIVIDUAL NEEDS

- Remember that the difficulty of the manipulative task for a given child should determine the number of equal boards set up for that child.
- In the area of number concept development, select the numeral cards used for a given child based on the learning needs of that child. For children who are having difficulty relating numerals to quantity, begin by using the same numeral on all the equal boards. Add and combine numerals as relationships are mastered using an ACQUISITION vs. MAINTENANCE* technique. For example, follow this pattern making sure each level is mastered before moving to the next:

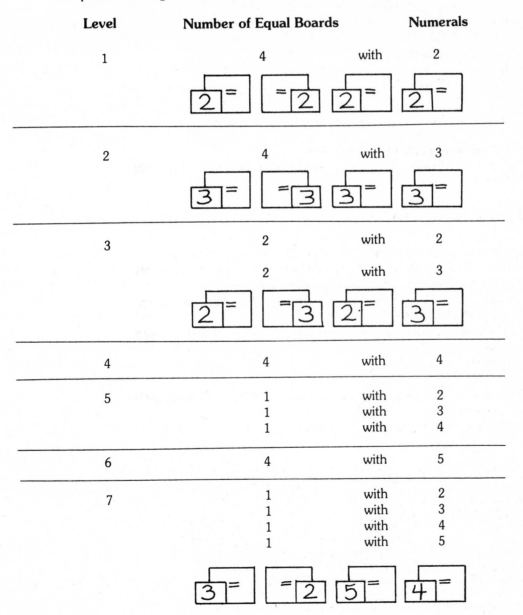

Level	Number of Equal Boards		Numerals
1	4	with	2
2	4	with	3
3	2	with	2
	2	with	3
4	4	with	4
5	1	with	2
	1	with	3
	1	with	4
6	4	with	5
7	1	with	2
	1	with	3
	1	with	4
	1	with	5

Marshmallow Equality

Continue this pattern of adding and combining.

*ACQUISITION vs. MAINTENANCE is a technique which can be applied to a variety of learning activities. Follow this pattern with any new material:

- teach one element of new material to mastery
- teach a second element of new material to mastery
- combine these two elements for practice
- teach a third element of new material to mastery
- combine these three elements for practice
- teach a fourth element of new material to mastery
- combine these four elements for practice
- continue to teach and combine for practice following this pattern.

For another application of the ACQUISITION vs. MAINTENANCE technique see **RAINBOW LAUNDRY.**

Plastic Egg Activities

MATERIALS IN COMMON

- 2-piece colored plastic eggs

FINDING MATERIALS

- Colored plastic eggs are widely available during the Easter season in discount stores, dime stores, drug store, and supermarkets. You will need at least one dozen in each of three sizes. Usually these come in six colors:

pink	blue	green
yellow	orange	purple

Small, Medium, or Large?

FOCUS ON

- matching colors
- developing manipulative skills
- classifying
- developing basic language concepts:
  *small, medium-sized, large, half,
  whole, separate, match*

MATERIALS

- 2-piece colored plastic eggs, one dozen in each of 3 sizes
- 3 egg cartons

To prepare egg cartons:

Make labels to fit inside the lid of each egg carton, using actual egg sizes in the drawings.

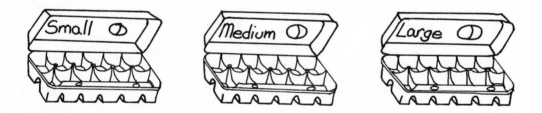

INDEPENDENT LEARNING CENTER

Place the three egg cartons at a learning center with three dozen plastic eggs. Have the child:

1. Separate all the plastic eggs, and mix the halves.
2. Put the eggs together, matching the colors of the two halves.
3. Put each egg into an egg carton according to size.

Point out that the large eggs will not all fit into the twelve sections and that some will need to go in the lid of the carton.

MEETING INDIVIDUAL NEEDS

- For a child who has difficulty with classifying by size, begin with two sizes — small and large. Add medium-sized eggs only when the child can sort by two sizes with ease.

Small, Medium, or Large?

- For a child who has difficulty dealing with size and color variables at the same time, separate the tasks:

  1. Provide one egg carton and one dozen eggs of a single size. Colors are to be matched without reference to size.
  2. Provide two or three egg cartons and eggs in two or three sizes. Ask the child to put the eggs together and sort them by size. Do not require color matching.

- For a child who has difficulty with the manipulative task of fitting the halves together, provide practice with other two-part materials such as:

  boxes with separate tops
  jars with lids
  margarine containers with tops
  cans with plastic covers.

- If a child tries to fit the wrong halves together, point out that he must find one egg half with a ridge and one egg half without a ridge before the halves will fit together. This gives the child a verbal cue for the visual component of the task.

Scrambled Eggs

FOCUS ON

- developing manipulative skills
- using tactile-kinesthetic information
- sequencing a task
- developing basic language concepts:
  small, medium-sized, large, half, whole,
  separate, inside, other, close

MATERIALS

- two-piece plastic eggs, one dozen in each of three sizes
- one empty egg carton
- blindfold (see Appendix B)
- box lid or tray

GROUP INSTRUCTION

1. Separate all three dozen eggs into halves, and spread them on the table or floor.
2. Seat children in a circle around the eggs.

To play **Scrambled Eggs:**

1. Have each child select:

   two small halves
   two medium-sized halves
   two large halves

2. Challenge each child to fit all these halves together to make *one* large egg.
3. Let the children help each other unscramble this problem!

Scrambled Eggs

Solution: Fit small halves together. Fit medium-sized halves together with small egg inside. Fit large halves together with medium-sized egg inside. Six halves = ◐

4. Encourage conversation about the task. Model use of the basic language concepts for the children.

"This is one large half."
"This is the other large half."
"This is a medium-sized egg with a small egg inside."
"The medium-sized egg fits inside the large halves."
"The large halves fit together to make a large whole egg."
"If I separate all my eggs, I have six halves."

INDEPENDENT LEARNING CENTER I

Provide one empty egg carton and three dozen two-piece plastic eggs. Have the child:

1. Separate the eggs into halves.
2. "Scramble" the egg halves.
3. Unscramble all three dozen eggs so they will fit into the one egg carton!

INDEPENDENT LEARNING CENTER II

Provide a blindfold, box lid or tray, and one large egg with a medium-sized and a small egg inside. Have the child:

1. Separate the one large egg into six halves, placing them in a box lid or on a tray.
2. Close his eyes, and put on the blindfold.
3. Fit the six halves together again into one large egg.

MEETING INDIVIDUAL NEEDS

- To simplify these activities, begin with only two egg sizes, adding the third size when children are successful with two.
- Be aware that some children may need step-by-step modeling of the required sequence. (Always allow time first for the child to discover the sequence.) Modeling procedure:

Scrambled Eggs

1. Provide two separate sets of six egg halves.
2. Verbalize and demonstrate fitting small egg halves together to make a whole egg.
3. Wait for the child to imitate this model, including the verbalization.
4. Physically assist the child by guiding his hands to the correct pieces, if necessary, to prevent an error.
5. Immediately reinforce the child's correct response with praise!
6. Verbalize and demonstrate fitting medium-sized egg halves together to make a whole egg with the small egg inside.
7. Repeat steps 3, 4, and 5.
8. Repeat with large egg halves.

- Use BACKWARD CHAINING* as another technique to help a child who is unable to accomplish the sequencing task independently.

Step 1. Have the child observe while you verbalize and demonstrate:

  - Fit small halves together to make a whole egg.
  - Fit medium-sized halves together with small egg inside.
  - Fit this medium-sized egg into *one* large half.

Hand this large half to the child with the other large half, and ask him to complete the large egg.

Continue to verbalize and demonstrate as for Step 1, working backward through the task. Separate all six pieces before beginning each step.

	Teacher hands child:	**Child completes task with:**
Step 2.	Medium-sized egg with small egg inside	Two large halves
Step 3.	Medium-sized half with small egg inside	Two large halves One medium-sized half
Step 4.	Small whole egg	Two large halves Two medium-sized halves
Step 5.	Nothing	All six halves

- If a child tries to fit the wrong halves together in the activity, Independent Learning Center II, ask him to feel for a ridge around the edge. Tell him he must find one egg half with a ridge and one egg half without a ridge before the halves will fit together. This gives him a verbal cue for the tactile-kinesthetic component of the task.

* BACKWARD CHAINING is appropriate for use with a variety of tasks. It builds in practice of each part of a task already learned, introduces only one new part of the task at a time, and allows the child to experience the satisfaction of task completion after each step.

Egg Puzzles

FOCUS ON

- developing manipulative skills
- recognizing and naming colors
- following directions
- giving directions
- understanding and using multiple attributes
- understanding and using negatives
- developing basic language concepts:
    *small, medium-sized, large, half, whole,
    separate, inside*

MATERIALS

- two-piece colored plastic eggs, one dozen in each of three sizes

GROUP INSTRUCTION

1. Ask a child to separate all three dozen eggs into halves and spread them on the table or floor.
2. Seat children in a circle around the eggs.
3. Discuss the eggs in terms of half, whole, size, and color.

To play **Egg Puzzles:**

1. Give a direction.
2. Call on one child, or the group, to carry out the direction. Not all directions can be used for a group, because there are only six eggs of each color and two eggs of each color-size combination. Appropriate directions for groups of 7 to 12 are marked with an asterisk(*).
3. Use directions which gradually increase in both length and complexity. Use the following examples as patterns to provide practice at each level as appropriate for each child.

    One-step direction, one attribute

    - *Make an egg that is whole.
    - *Find an egg half.

    One-step direction, two attributes

    - Make an egg that is whole and yellow.
    - *Make an egg that is whole and large.
    - *Find an egg half that is pink.
    - *Find an egg half that is medium-sized.

Egg Puzzles

One-step direction, three attributes

- Make an egg that is whole, small, and blue.
- Find an egg half that is large and purple.
- Make a whole egg that is half yellow and half green.

Two-step direction, one attribute

- *Find an egg half. Hide it inside an egg that is whole.

Two-step direction, two attributes

- *Make an egg that is whole and small. Hide it inside an egg that is whole and large.
- Find an egg half that is orange. Hide it inside an egg that is whole and green.
- *Find an egg half that is small. Put it inside an egg half that is medium-sized.
- Make an egg that is whole and pink. Hide it inside an egg that is whole and medium-sized.
- *Find an egg half that is pink. Fit it together with an egg half that is blue.

Two-step direction, three attributes

- Make an egg that is whole, medium-sized, and green. Hide it inside an egg that is whole, large, and blue.
- Find an egg half that is small and orange. Fit it together with an egg half that is small and purple.

4. When children can follow these directions with ease on a given level, try working with negatives at that level.

One-step direction, one attribute

- *Show me an egg that is not whole.

One-step direction, two attributes

- *Make an egg that is whole and not yellow.
- *Make an egg that is whole and not large.
- *Find an egg half that is not blue.
- *Find an egg half that is not small.

One-step direction, three attributes

- *Make an egg that is whole and not small or purple.
- *Find an egg half that is not large or pink.

5. When giving group directions, ask children to see how many different ways there are to correctly follow the directions.

Egg Puzzles

6. When children can follow directions easily on a given level, have them give directions to each other. Practice in giving directions is very important, but first the teacher must model the required language patterns.

MEETING INDIVIDUAL NEEDS

- Remember to place attribute information at the end of the sentence as the above patterns illustrate. This is important because some children with language deficits *key* on the last words heard and retain only those words. One way to meet the needs of these children is to keep essential information at the end of the sentence.
- For a child who has trouble with the manipulative task of fitting the egg halves together, provide practice with the Plastic Egg activity, **Small, Medium, or Large?**
- Choose the child(ren) who is to respond *after* a direction is given. This is important as a strategy for maintaining the attention of each child to each direction.

    "Find an egg ——————, Jimmy."
    "Make an egg ——————, everyone!"

Egg Hunt Surprise

FOCUS ON

- matching colors
- recognizing and naming colors
- remembering multiple attributes
- developing basic language concepts:
    small, large, inside, open, down

MATERIALS

- two-piece colored plastic eggs, one dozen large and one dozen small
- tagboard cue cards
- surprises

To prepare cue cards:

1. Cut three sheets of tagboard into quarters to make 12 cards.
2. On each card draw two egg shapes, one large and one small. Make the sizes identical to actual egg sizes.
3. Fill in the egg shapes with colors to match the colors of the plastic eggs. Use two different colors on each card. Cover with clear contact.

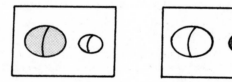

For surprises, provide 24 items:

raisins	happy faces
popped corn	gummed seals
bing cherries	charms
cherry tomatoes	pennies
grapes	peanuts in the shell
animal crackers	pistachio nuts in the shell
small pretzels	balloons
carrot sticks	jelly beans

Helpful hint

- Materials as described are sufficient for a group of six children.

Egg Hunt Surprise

GROUP INSTRUCTION

Try this egg hunt with a difference!

1. Place a surprise inside each egg.
2. Hide the eggs.

To play **Egg Hunt Surprise:**

1. Give each child one cue card to study and remember.
2. Signal the beginning of the hunt! Children leave cue cards face up on the table where they may return to look again, if necessary.
3. Help children compare eggs they find with cue cards. They may keep only eggs identical to cue cards in both size and color.
4. Allow each child to open the egg and find the surprise!
5. Pass out a second cue card to each child.
6. This time the card is placed *face down* during the hunt!

MEETING INDIVIDUAL NEEDS

- If children have difficulty remembering both size and color, let them begin by taking cue cards with them for reference as they hunt.
- Another way to help children who are having difficulty is to verbalize the multiple attributes of the eggs. "You are looking for one egg that is big and green and one egg that is little and yellow." Ask the child to verbalize. "Which eggs are you looking for?"
- If the children are having difficulty, begin with cue cards showing only one egg.
- Permit groups of able children to move to cue cards showing three eggs — large, medium-sized, and small.

In An Eggshell

FOCUS ON

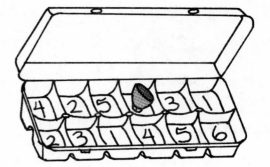

- recognizing and naming colors
- matching object to picture
- counting
- naming numerals
- using left-to-right progression
- using top-to-bottom progression
- remembering multiple attributes
- recognizing proper names
- developing basic language concepts:
    *small, medium-sized, large, same, different,
    alike, match, open, closed, inside, left, right, top,
    bottom, start, begin, stop, next, half, whole, above, below*

MATERIALS

- two-piece colored plastic eggs, one dozen in each of three sizes
- egg carton
- open-ended trail game board (see Appendix B)
- game markers with children's names (see Appendix B)
- name cards
- surprises

To prepare eggs:

1. Set aside 18 eggs, one of each size-color combination, for use on the open-ended trail game board.
2. Inside of 14 eggs, place cards with the names of children playing the game. Any given child may have his name inside more than one egg, the number depending on the size of the group playing.
3. Inside each of four eggs place *enough surprises for each child to have one* (or picture of surprise to be collected). See suggestions for surprises in the activity, **Egg Hunt Surprise**.

To prepare egg carton:

1. With a black marking pen, write two each of numerals 1-6 in the 12 sections of an egg carton.

2. Take one small-sized egg half from the eggs reserved for the game board, and place it in the egg carton.

To set up game board:

Take 18 egg halves, one of each size-color combination, and distribute them along the trails of the open-ended game board.

In An Eggshell

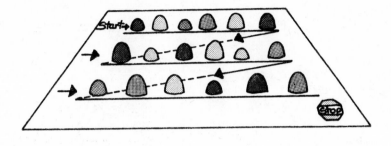

GROUP INSTRUCTION

1. Place the eggs away from the game in a spot where the game board is *not* visible.
2. Seat a group of children in front of (not around) the game board.
3. Discuss the game board in terms of:

   - Beginning at the START arrow
   - Moving from left to right
   - Moving from top to bottom
   - Ending at the STOP sign
   - Watching the arrows to help remember

4. Give each child a game marker.

To play **In An Eggshell,** have each child:

1. Turn the closed egg carton upside-down, and shake the egg half inside the carton.
2. Turn the egg carton right side up, and open it.
3. Read the numeral in the section containing the egg half.
4. Beginning at the START arrow, count this number of egg halves, and place game marker above the egg half indicated.
5. Name the size and color of this egg half.
6. Go to the whole eggs in another part of the room where the game board cannot be seen.
7. Choose the egg which is the same as the egg half.
8. Return to the group with the egg.
9. Compare the egg with the egg half below his marker.
10. If a correct match is made,

    - Open the egg.
    - Hold up the name (this child has the next turn).
    - Or share the surprise he has earned with all the players, then choose a child to have the next turn.
    - Remove the egg half below his marker from the game board.

11. If an incorrect match is made, again verbalize the size and color of the egg half, and return to exchange eggs.

69

In An Eggshell

MEETING INDIVIDUAL NEEDS

- If children cannot yet recognize their names, use different colored game markers. Color may then serve as a cue to name recognition.
- Remember that including a child who has won disfavor with his peer group may give him an opportunity to win a surprise for the entire group and receive positive reinforcement from his peers. Emphasize the fact that he won the surprise for everyone!
- If children have difficulty remembering both size and color, let them begin by taking a size or color cue card for reference as they go to choose an egg.

Miniature Clothing Activities

MATERIALS IN COMMON

- miniature clothing shapes
- colored clothespins
- clothesline

MAKING MATERIALS

To make miniature clothing shapes:

1. Collect fabric scraps in a variety of prints, patterns, and solid colors including different textures and weights. Avoid fabrics which tend to ravel easily.
2. Use patterns from Appendix A-4.
3. Pin a pattern to several layers of fabric.
4. Cut out.

BUYING MATERIALS

Assemble one set of colored clothespins. Choose either:

1. colored plastic spring clothespins
2. wood spring clothespins (spray paint in primary colors)
3. "any direction" round clothespins which come in assorted bright colors (see Appendix C).

HELPFUL HINTS

- Ask parents to save leftover scraps of fabric.
- When possible, choose fabric typical of the clothing item.

  jeans — denim   slips — nylon tricot   raincoat — plastic or vinyl

- Use a worn-out wool sock to make a sweater.
- Utilize old plastic or leather purses for belts and shoes.
- Cut around the bottom of a worn lace-trimmed slip incorporating the lace to fashion slips and half-slips.
- Use different fabric to differentiate shirt, sweater, and coat.
- To help identify a coat, add buttons with a magic marker.
- Hang the clothesline between two chairs, two door handles, two nails in the wall across a corner, or other suitable location low enough for a child to reach comfortably. It is important that the line be taut.

Laundry Mix-Up

FOCUS ON

- developing manipulative skills
- naming common clothing
- sequencing a task
- developing basic language concepts:
  *over, under, top, first, second, third,
  next, last, in order*

MATERIALS

- miniature clothing sets
- clothesline and clothespins
- envelopes

To prepare miniature clothing sets, make one set of clothes for each child. In each set, include three clothing items worn one on top of the other, such as:

men's undershorts	shirt	lady's underpants	undershirt
jeans	sweater	slacks	shirt
raincoat	coat	belt	jacket
men's undershorts	slip	men's undershorts	half-slip
jeans	dress	shorts	skirt
leather belt	apron	belt	belt
lady's underpants	slip	lady's underpants	sock
skirt	dress	long half-slip	shoe
apron	coat	long skirt	boot

Place each set in an envelope.

GROUP INSTRUCTION

1. Lay out a box of clothespins and the miniature clothing sets in envelopes. Put up a clothesline nearby.
2. Using one set of clothes, talk about the order in which these items of clothing must be put on. Place one clothing item on top of another as you discuss the sequence involved in getting dressed. For example, in a set including a shirt, jacket, and undershirt, the order would be *undershirt, shirt, jacket.*

Laundry Mix-Up

3. Pick up the layered set with the outside layer of clothing on top, or facing you. Hang on the clothesline.
4. Have each child in turn:

   - Choose an envelope.
   - Name the clothing.
   - Put the clothing in order.
   - Hang the clothing on the clothesline.

5. Encourage the children to talk about each response. Everyone enjoys the fun when somebody discovers one cannot wear underpants on top of a skirt!

INDEPENDENT LEARNING CENTER

For a challenging independent activity, lay out clothing envelopes. Selecting one envelope at a time, have the child:

1. Remove the clothes from the envelope.
2. Put the clothes in order.
3. Hang them on the clothesline.

When all clothing sets are hanging on the line, check them for sequence.

MEETING INDIVIDUAL NEEDS

- If the sequencing task is too difficult for a child, give him a set with only two items of clothing.
- If a child will be uncomfortable sequencing clothes typically associated with the opposite sex, let him work only with those sets appropriate to his sex.

Laundromat

FOCUS ON

- developing manipulative skills
- classifying
- developing basic language concepts:
    light, dark, other

MATERIALS

- miniature clothing shapes
- two miniature laundry baskets
- miniature washer and dryer
- clothesline and clothespins

To prepare miniature clothing shapes:

Choose miniature clothing shapes in two categories:

1. Fabrics in solid colors — dark shades
2. Fabrics in solid colors — pastel shades

To prepare miniature laundry baskets:

Purchase two small baskets such as wicker bread baskets.

To make miniature washer and dryer:

1. Secure two square gift boxes.
2. Cut openings and use marking pen to draw on details.

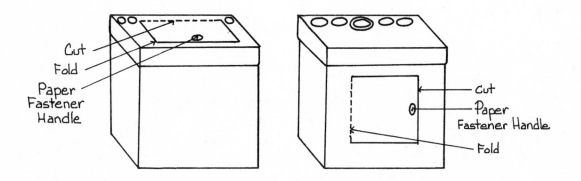

Laundromat

INDEPENDENT LEARNING CENTER

Set up clothesline and provide clothes, baskets, clothespins, washer, and dryer at a learning center.

1. Ask the child to pretend he is sorting laundry. All the light colored clothes go in one basket. All the dark colored clothes go in the other basket.
2. Have the child repeat the instructions.
3. Allow the child to sort the clothing independently.

4. When the task is completed, ask, "Which basket has clothes that are light colored? dark colored?"
5. After successfully classifying clothes into light and dark, allow the child unstructured time for fun with the clothes, baskets, washer, dryer, clothesline, and clothespins.

MEETING INDIVIDUAL NEEDS

- Observe children during unstructured activity time to ascertain any inability to organize or sequence events. Use this information to program future activities which emphasize sequential tasks.

Design for Decision

FOCUS ON

- naming common fabric designs
- classifying
- developing basic language concepts:
    same, different

MATERIALS

- miniature clothing shapes
- 6 fabric design cue cards
- open-ended spinner (see Appendix B)
- 6 boxes

To make fabric design cue cards:

1. Cut one 3½" x 5½" piece of fabric for each design category:

solid color	checks
print	stripes
plaid	polka dots

2. Sew or glue fabric to 4" x 6" tagboard cards.

Helpful hints

- Use pinking shears for cutting fabric.
- Try pattern adhesive, which can be purchased in a spray can at fabric stores, to hold fabric in place securely on the card while it is being stitched.
- Sew fabric to cards using a zigzag sewing machine.

GROUP INSTRUCTION

1. Select clothing shapes to represent each of the six categories on the fabric design cue cards.
2. Place one cue card in each section of the open-ended spinner and spread out the clothing shapes nearby.

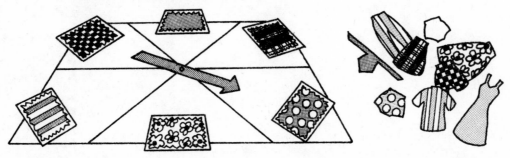

Design for Decision

3. Have each child in turn:

   - Spin the spinner.
   - Name the fabric design using sentence patterns such as, "This fabric is a print," or "This fabric has checks."
   - Choose a clothing shape with the same fabric design.

INDEPENDENT LEARNING CENTER

Set up the cue cards and boxes, and have children sort the miniature clothing by the six fabric design categories.

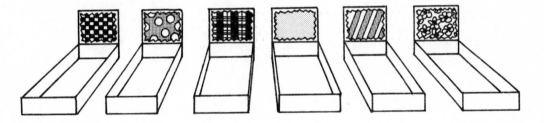

MEETING INDIVIDUAL NEEDS

- For those children who have difficulty labeling the category *solid color*, say, "It does not have stripes; it does not have polka dots; etc. It is the same all over. It is a solid color."
- For children who have difficulty with sentence patterns, avoid presenting two patterns simultaneously. Have these children play with only three fabric design categories. Put two cue cards on the spinner for each category. Keep sentence patterns consistent:

solid color	"This fabric *is* a solid color."
print	"This fabric *is* a print."
plaid	"This fabric *is* a plaid."

  or

checks	"This fabric *has* checks."
stripes	"This fabric *has* stripes."
polka dots	"This fabric *has* polka dots."

- Remember that the classification task required by including six categories at the Independent Learning Center may be too complex for some children. The most difficult discriminations are between the stripes, check, and plaid categories. Initially, include only one of these, adding categories as the child improves his skill.

What Are You Wearing?

FOCUS ON

- developing manipulative skills
- naming common clothing
- naming common fabric designs
- classifying
- recognizing proper names
- developing basic language concepts:
  top, bottom, same, different, below

MATERIALS

- miniature clothing shapes
- clothesline and clothespins
- six fabric design cue cards as for **Design for Decision**
- six pocket cards as for **Pocket Activities**
- six name cards for each child
- thumbtacks

GROUP INSTRUCTION

1. Hang clothesline and provide clothespins.
2. Lay out assorted clothing shapes illustrating the six fabric designs on the cue cards (solid color, print, plaid, checks, stripes, polka dots).
3. Help the children name the fabric designs on the cue cards.
4. Place the cue cards face down in a pile.

To play **What Are You Wearing?** have each child in turn:

1. Take a cue card from the top of the pile.
2. Name the fabric design on the cue card: "This fabric is a solid color." "This fabric has polka dots."
3. Choose a clothing shape in the fabric design category on the cue card.
4. Name the clothing: "This is a shirt." "This is a dress."
5. Name the clothing fabric design: "The shirt is a solid color." "The dress has polka dots."
6. Hang the clothing shape on the clothesline with a clothespin.
7. Look for a child wearing clothing in the fabric design category on the cue card.
8. Name both the fabric design and the clothing, or report, "No one is wearing clothing that has polka dots."
9. Place the cue card on the bottom of the pile.

What Are You Wearing?

INDEPENDENT LEARNING CENTER

1. Set up a bulletin board as a learning center.

   - Divide the board into six sections.
   - Place one pocket card at the bottom of each section.
   - Put a set of name cards, one for each child, in each pocket.
   - Post one design cue card at the top of each section.
   - Provide thumbtacks.

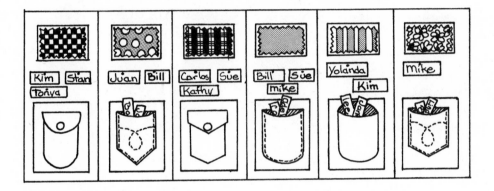

2. Daily ask each child to post his name below the fabric design cue card in each section which corresponds to an item of clothing he is wearing.
3. Return names to pockets at the end of the day.

MEETING INDIVIDUAL NEEDS

   - For children who have difficulty naming fabric designs, play **Design for Decision** until they have mastered this skill.
   - For those children who need help with orientation of their name cards, draw a dot at the top of the name card indicating where to hang the card with a thumbtack.

Counting Clothes

FOCUS ON

- developing manipulative skills
- naming common clothing
- counting
- using one-to-one correspondence
- recognizing and naming numerals
- relating numerals to quantity
- classifying
- developing basic language concepts:
  long, short, side, right

MATERIALS

- miniature clothing sets
- clothing-numeral cue cards
- clothesline and clothespins

To prepare miniature clothing sets:

Assemble ten sets, such as the following, and include one or more extra items in each set. Vary the number of extras from set to set.

1. one short belt
2. two long dresses
3. three short pants
4. four long sleeve shirts
5. five long skirts
6. six long pants
7. seven short dresses
8. eight short sleeve shirts
9. nine short skirts
10. ten long belts

To prepare clothing-numeral cue cards:

1. Cut one of each clothing shape from tagboard using patterns from Appendix A-4.
2. Put a numeral for each set on the corresponding tagboard clothing shape.

INDEPENDENT LEARNING CENTER

1. Hang the clothing-numeral cue cards in numerical order on the clothesline, allowing space to the right of each card for the set of clothing.

Counting Clothes

2. Ask the child to name the clothing shape and the numeral on each card. Have the child hang clothing shapes on the right side of each cue card, using the cue card to tell:

   - which clothing shapes to hang
   - how many of each clothing shape to hang.

MEETING INDIVIDUAL NEEDS

- To simplify this task, begin with a few cue cards and gradually increase the number of cards used.
- When cooperative interaction needs emphasis, let two children work together on this activity.
- If a child is not ready to relate numerals to quantity, prepare additional cue cards as illustrated. Let him take the cue cards down and lay clothing shapes on them, using one-to-one correspondence if necessary.

- For another way to help a child who is having difficulty relating numerals to quantity, use a longer clothesline and hang either set of clothing-numeral cards to allow space for one clothespin on each clothing shape. This will emphasize the number of clothing shapes in each set.

Rainbow Laundry

FOCUS ON

- developing manipulative skills
- recognizing colors
- matching colors
- attending to internal detail
- developing basic language concepts:
  same, different, around

MATERIALS

- miniature clothing shapes
- colored clothespins
- clothesline
- colored paper plates

INDEPENDENT LEARNING CENTER

1. Lay out a box of clothespins (one color only) and a box of miniature clothes. Include miniature clothes with the selected color in a variety of prints and patterns, for example, if red is selected, have the child:
   - Find a clothing shape with red in it.
   - Hang this clothing shape on the clothesline with a red clothespin.
   - Continue until all shapes with any red in them are hanging on the line.
2. Repeat the activity with a second color (for example, blue).
3. Repeat the activity with colors 1 and 2 combined. (red and blue)
4. Repeat with a third color. (for example, yellow)
5. Repeat with colors 1, 2, and 3 combined. (red, blue, yellow)
6. Continue introducing and combining colors following the above pattern.

MEETING INDIVIDUAL NEEDS

- Give a child who has difficulty with this task clothes in solid colors only.
- Since some children need a variety of matching activities for each new color presented, use the clothespins with colored paper plates to structure another set of activities. Focus on one color at a time by providing one plate in a single color and clothespins in several colors.

   Have the child:
   1. Find all the clothespins that are the same color as the plate.
   2. Clip these clothespins around the plate.

   When you are ready to focus on yellow, surprise the child with Leo-the-Lion.
- Use the above colored plate activity for a child who needs additional practice manipulating clothespins.

Small Box Activities

MATERIALS IN COMMON

- small boxes with removable lids

FINDING MATERIALS

- Ask parents, relatives, neighbors, and friends to save small boxes for you.

- Collect jewelry boxes in assorted sizes, since they are ideal for many of these activities. Get jewelry stores or jewelry departments to donate the boxes you need or sell them to you at a nominal cost.

Get It Together

FOCUS ON

- developing manipulative skills
- matching objects
- sequencing a task
- developing basic language concepts:
  *separate, top, bottom, every, few, inside,
  big, little, small, medium-sized, large*

MATERIALS

- assorted small boxes, each a different size or shape

Helpful hint

When selecting boxes, watch for those with

- similar but different sizes and shapes
- a variety of textures
- different color tops and bottoms
- colorful pictures or decorations on the tops.

INDEPENDENT LEARNING CENTER

To play **Get It Together,** Task I, place assorted small boxes at a learning center.
Have the child:

1. Separate the top and the bottom of every box.

    - Put all the tops in one pile.
    - Put all the bottoms in another pile.

2. Find a top and a bottom that fit together.
3. Continue until all boxes are put back together.

To play **Get It Together,** Task II, place assorted small boxes at a learning
center. Have the child:

1. Separate the top and bottom of every box.

    - Put all the tops in one pile.
    - Put all the bottoms in another pile.

2. Match tops and bottoms to put boxes back together. This time, put boxes
   one inside another whenever they will fit.

Get It Together

Challenge the child to end up with as few boxes as possible.

MEETING INDIVIDUAL NEEDS

- Be aware that when the top and bottom of a box are different in color or texture, it is more difficult to put the box together. In this case the color or texture becomes a *distractor*, which adds challenge to the task. Include these boxes for children who are ready to work with them successfully.

- If a child has difficulty with sequencing in Task II, choose boxes that can be fit one inside the other, and follow a BACKWARD CHAINING* procedure. An example of BACKWARD CHAINING for a three box set:

    Step 1. Have the child observe while you verbalize and demonstrate:

    - fit top and bottom of smallest box together
    - fit top and bottom of medium-sized box together with smallest box inside
    - fit this box into bottom of largest box.

    Hand this large box bottom to the child with the remaining box top and ask her to finish putting the box together.

Continue to verbalize and demonstrate as for Step 1, working backward through the task. Separate all six pieces before beginning each step.

	Teacher hands child:	Child completes task with:
Step 2.	Medium-sized box with small box inside	Top and bottom of large box
Step 3.	Bottom of medium-sized box with small box inside	Top and bottom of large box, top and bottom of medium-sized box
Step 4.	Small box	Top and bottom of both large and medium-sized boxes.
Step 5.	Nothing	All six box parts.

*BACKWARD CHAINING is appropriate for use with a variety of tasks. It builds in practice of each part of a task already learned, introduces only one new part of the task at a time, and allows the child to experience the satisfaction of task completion after each step.

If The Top Fits

FOCUS ON

- developing manipulative skills
- recognizing numerals
- relating numerals to quantity
- developing basic language concepts:
  open, closed, inside, top, bottom

MATERIALS

- 10 small boxes, each a *different* but similar size and shape
- gummed seals

To prepare small boxes:

1. Write the numerals 1-10 inside the bottom of each box.
2. Glue gummed seals, in quantities to match the numerals, inside the top of each box.

INDEPENDENT LEARNING CENTER

Spread the open boxes, insides showing, with tops and bottoms scrambled. Have the child:

1. Choose a numeral (box bottom).
2. Find the corresponding number of seals (box top).
3. Check these choices by fitting the box top and the box bottom together.
4. If the box fits together, the choice was correct. If the box does not fit together, try again.
5. Continue until all boxes are closed.

MEETING INDIVIDUAL NEEDS

- When giving instructions for the independent learning task, emphasize any of the basic language concepts indicated.
- If a child is unable to relate numerals to quantity, add a set of *different* seals as a cue below the numeral.

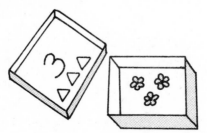

Deep or Shallow?

FOCUS ON

- using tactile-kinesthetic information
- recognizing weight differences
- relating weights to objects
- relating sounds to objects
- remembering things seen
- using left-to-right progression
- using top-to-bottom progression
- recognizing proper names
- developing basic language concepts:
    *deep, shallow, inside, top, begin, start, follow, stop,
    above, open, closed, pair, empty, full, light, heavy*

MATERIALS

- six deep boxes, six shallow boxes
- 12 objects to go inside boxes
- 12 object picture cards (see Appendix A-5)
- open-ended trail game board (see Appendix B)
- deep-shallow die
- game markers with children's names (see Appendix B)

To prepare boxes:

Put these objects into deep boxes:

apple	small child's pair of shoes
empty ½ pt. milk carton	ball (approximately 3″)
cup	can of soup (unopened)

Put these objects into shallow boxes:

birthday card	knife, fork, and spoon
two keys	three pencils
small child's pair of mittens	scissors

(Choose shallow boxes which none of the deep objects could fit into.)

To make deep-shallow die:

1. Purchase a 12″ x 12″ x 3″ foam pad, available for under 50¢ at building-material, sporting-goods, fabric, and surplus stores.
2. Cut a 3″ square using a sharp knife. (An electric knife works beautifully.)
3. Using sharp pointed scissors, cut out deep holes, off center, on three surfaces.
4. Cut out shallow holes, centered, on the remaining three surfaces.

Deep or Shallow?

GROUP INSTRUCTION

1. Place the deep boxes on one side of the open-ended trail game board and the shallow boxes on the other side of the board. Have game markers and the deep-shallow die available.
2. Seat children in front of (*not* around) the game board.
3. Help the children name the object picture cards as you place them along the four trails on the open-ended game board.

4. Tell the children these are pictures of objects which are hidden inside the boxes. Mention that the soup can is full and the milk carton is empty.
5. Talk about the differences between the boxes.

> "This box is deep." (Remove the cover from one deep box and show inside.)
> "All of these boxes are deep."

Repeat with the shallow boxes.

6. Show the deep-shallow die.

> "This hole is deep."
> "This hole is shallow."

Allow the children to feel inside the deep and shallow holes.

7. Say, "We're going to play a game about deep and shallow."

Deep or Shallow?

To play **Deep or Shallow?,** have each child:

1. Roll the deep-shallow die and identify the top hole, "This hole is deep (shallow)."
2. Follow the game board trail with a game marker until he reaches a picture of an object which goes with a deep (shallow) box as indicated by the die. He must decide, "Does this object need a deep box? Would it fit in a shallow box?"
3. Place the game marker above this picture.
4. Go to the group of boxes (deep or shallow) as indicated by the die and try to select the box containing this pictured object. In making his choice, the child may:

    - Feel the weight of the closed box
    - Shake the closed box to listen to the sound.

5. Open the box to check.
6. If choice was correct, remove the object picture card, retaining it until the end of the game, and remove the box from play.

MEETING INDIVIDUAL NEEDS

- Since the game becomes easier as the number of boxes to choose from decreases, begin the game with the most capable children to build in a better success opportunity for children you predict will have difficulty.
- To make the game more challenging, leave boxes in play after correct choices.
- If children cannot yet recognize their names, use different colored game markers. Color may then serve as a cue to name recognition.

Penny Wise

FOCUS ON

- matching sounds
- using tactile-kinesthetic information
- recognizing weight differences
- remembering things heard
- counting
- using one-to-one correspondence
- recognizing and naming numerals
- relating numerals to quantity
- estimating
- developing basic language concepts:
    equal, same, different, open, closed, inside, zero,
    empty, in order, least, most, front, light, heavy

MATERIALS

- 10 small boxes, identical size and shape
- 55 pennies
- numeral cue cards
- game tokens
- equal boards (see Appendix B)

To prepare small boxes:

1. Put pennies inside boxes as indicated for each game:

    Box 1 — 1 penny
    Box 2 — 2 pennies
        etc.
    Box 10 — 10 pennies

2. Put a small Roman numeral on the bottom of each box for teacher use when setting up materials.

To make numeral cue cards:

1. Cut ten 3″ x 12″ tagboard strips.
2. Fold each strip to make a 3″ x 6″ card.
3. Put a numeral on the front of the card. Make one card for each numeral 1-10.
4. Put the same numeral and a corresponding number of penny-pictures inside each card. To make penny pictures, draw around a penny or use a penny coin stamp (see Appendix C).

 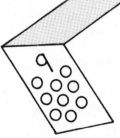

Penny Wise

5. Clip each card together at the bottom.

To prepare game tokens, select one of the following game token suggestions:

1. Use pennies from play money.
2. Use a penny coin stamp on tagboard. Cut out pennies.
3. Use a coin stamp during the game to stamp pennies directly on the back of each child's hand.
4. Give each child a blank card and let him stamp a penny, as earned, on the card.

GROUP INSTRUCTION

To play **Penny Wise,** Game I (Equal Quantities):

1. Provide six boxes: two each of Boxes 1, 5, 9
2. Seat children around boxes.
3. Follow this procedure for each pair of boxes:

   - Open the two boxes.
   - Count the pennies.
   - Explain, "The boxes have an *equal* number of pennies. They both have _____ pennies."
   - Close the boxes and shake them, commenting that they sound the same.
   - Hold one box in each hand and test the weight, commenting that they weigh the same.
   - Allow each child a turn to shake and test the weight of the two boxes.

4. Have each child in turn:

   - Choose one box, shake, and test the weight.
   - Shake and test the weight of the remaining boxes to find the one with an *equal* number of pennies.
   - Open the two boxes and compare.

     Decide (estimate) whether they are equal.
     Count the pennies to find out if they are equal.

   - Close and return the boxes.

5. Reinforce each correct response immediately with one game token.
6. Mix the boxes after each turn.

Penny Wise

Increase to eight and ten boxes in Game I as the children are ready for a more challenging task. Select boxes as for the numeral games which follow.

To play **Penny Wise,** Game II (Numerals 1, 5, 9 or 2, 6, 10):

1. Provide three boxes: Boxes 1, 5, 9 or Boxes 2, 6, 10. Provide the three corresponding numeral cue cards.
2. Seat children around boxes and face-down cue cards.
3. Follow this procedure for each box.

   - Open box.
   - Count pennies.
   - Close box.
   - Ask each child to shake the box and test its weight.

4. Have each child in turn:

   - Choose a card, and name the numeral.
   - Shake the boxes, trying to find the box with the indicated number of pennies.
   - Open the chosen box, and decide (estimate) whether the choice was correct.
   - Count the pennies inside the box.
   - Close and return the box and cue card.

5. Reinforce each correct response immediately with one game token.
6. Mix the boxes and cue cards after each turn.

Follow instructions for Game II when playing Games III, IV, or V, substituting box numerals as indicated.

Penny Wise, Game III (Numerals 1, 3, 5, 9 or 1, 4, 6, 10)
Penny Wise, Game IV (Numerals 1, 3, 5, 7, 9 or 2, 4, 6, 8, 10)
Penny Wise, Game V (Numerals 1, 2, 3, 4, 5)

To play **Penny Wise,** Game VI (Zero):

Teach the basic language concept zero by adding an empty box or boxes to any of the preceding games.

Penny Wise

INDEPENDENT LEARNING CENTER I

Provide 3, 4, or 5 equal boards with 3, 4, or 5 pairs of boxes. Provide only as many choices as the child is ready to handle successfully. Have the child:

1. Choose one box and shake it.
2. Shake the remaining boxes to find the box with an equal number of pennies.
3. Place boxes on an equal board.
4. Check the completed task by:

   - Opening each pair of boxes and counting.
   - Matching the pennies, one at a time from each box, using one-to-one correspondence if necessary.

INDEPENDENT LEARNING CENTER II

Provide boxes and numeral cue cards as for Games II, III, IV, or V. Remove paper clips from cue cards and stand them from least to most at a learning center. Have the child:

1. Put the boxes in order from least to most by shaking them and placing them in front of the numeral cue cards.
2. Check the completed task by:

   - Opening each box and counting.
   - Laying the pennies on the penny pictures, using one-to-one correspondence if necessary.

MEETING INDIVIDUAL NEEDS

- For children who do not relate numerals to quantity with ease, set up the Independent Learning Center II activity with numeral cue cards inside out.

Don't Take It Light-ly!

FOCUS ON

- using tactile-kinesthetic information
- recognizing weight differences
- giving directions
- using multiple attributes
- developing basic language concepts:
  light-heavy, light-dark, same, different

MATERIALS

- 8 small boxes, identical size, shape, and color

To prepare small boxes:

1. Put a small Zip-Lock bag of sand inside each of four boxes.
2. Leave four boxes empty.
3. Tie two lightweight boxes and two heavy boxes with light blue ribbon.
4. Tie two lightweight boxes and two heavy boxes with dark blue ribbon.

GROUP INSTRUCTION

To play **Don't Take It Light-ly!**, Game I:

1. Seat children around the eight boxes.
2. Hand a light and a heavy box with the same color ribbon to one child.
3. Ask, "Are these boxes the same weight?"
4. Identify, "The weight of this box is light."
      "The weight of this box is heavy."
5. Repeat with each child.
6. Have each child in turn: "Find a box that is light." "Find a box that is heavy."
7. When children can follow directions easily, allow them a turn to give directions to each other.

To play **Don't Take It Light-ly!**, Game II:

1. Seat children around the eight boxes.
2. Discuss two boxes, one light color and one dark color ribbon.
3. Say, "The ribbons are both blue. Are the blue colors the same?"
4. Identify: "The blue color of this ribbon is light."
      "The blue color of this ribbon is dark."
5. Have each child in turn: "Find a ribbon that is light (dark) blue."
6. When children can follow directions easily, allow them a turn to give directions to each other.

Don't Take It Light-ly!

To play **Don't Take It Light-ly!**, Game III:

1. Seat children around the eight boxes.
2. Give directions combining all the concepts.

   One attribute:
   "Find a box that is heavy."
   "Find a box with a ribbon that is a light blue color."
   "Find a box that is lightweight."
   "Find a box with a ribbon that is a dark blue color."

   Two attributes:
   "Find a box that is lightweight with a ribbon that is a dark blue color."
   "Find a box that is heavy with a ribbon that is a light blue color."

3. When children can follow directions easily, allow them a turn to give directions to each other.

MEETING INDIVIDUAL NEEDS

- If children are ready, move from one game to another during the same lesson. For other children, plan Games I, II, and III for successive days.
- For children who are having difficulty, provide a variety of materials to illustrate the concepts being taught.
- For independent learning center ideas which correlate with **Don't Take It Light-ly!**, see **Which Weigh?** (light, heavy), **Laundromat** (light, dark).

What's Inside?

FOCUS ON

- developing manipulative skills
- matching objects
- remembering things seen
- developing basic language concepts:
    inside, open, closed, same, different, alike, match, pair

MATERIALS

- 12 small boxes
- pairs of identical small objects
- game board

To prepare small boxes:

1. Select six pairs of small objects.
2. Put one object in each of the 12 boxes.

Suggestions for pairs of small objects:

keys	charms and novelties (see Appendix C)
mittens and gloves	balloons in assorted shapes and sizes
miniature clothing shapes	assorted wrapped candies
halves of colored plastic eggs	gummed seals
miniature toys	assorted nuts in the shell
	earrings

To make game board:

Use 22" x 28" poster board and marking pen to make the following game board:

GROUP INSTRUCTION

Play **What's Inside?** like the game "Concentration" — but with a special twist!

1. Seat children in a circle around game board with one closed box on each square. Have extra pairs of small objects within reach.
2. Have each child in turn:

What's Inside?

- Choose two boxes to open, trying to find a pair of identical objects.
- Close lids on incorrect choices returning these boxes to the same game board squares. (Be sure all children see contents before lids are replaced.)
- Remove objects from the boxes on correct choices, and retain them until the end of the game.

3. Replace the small objects each time a pair is correctly selected following this procedure:

- Have several extra pairs available.
- Select two different pairs when a match is made.
- Put one object from each pair into the empty boxes. The remaining two objects do not go into play until another match is made, and two more empty boxes become available.
- Repeat this procedure so that no pair is put into play at the same time.

MEETING INDIVIDUAL NEEDS

- Decrease the difficulty level of **What's Inside?** by decreasing the number of boxes used. Increase the challenge of the task by increasing the number of boxes used.

Flip Your Lid

FOCUS ON

- developing manipulative skills
- naming common objects
- relating part to whole
- counting
- developing basic language concepts:
  top, bottom, inside, outside, match,
  open, closed, same, different

MATERIALS

- 15 small boxes, the same size and shape
- open-ended spinner (see Appendix B)

To prepare small boxes:

Use pictures from Appendix A-6 to make 15 small boxes into part-whole boxes.

Identical pictures to glue inside box top and inside box bottom		*Picture to glue outside box top*	*Picture to glue outside box bottom*
Box 1	letter	stamp	address
Box 2	house	roof	door
Box 3	telephone	dial	receiver
Box 4	clock	hands	numerals
Box 5	tree	leaves	trunk
Box 6	coat	sleeve	collar
Box 7	lamp	shade	bulb
Box 8	bicycle	wheels	handlebars
Box 9	flower	petals	stem
Box 10	hammer	head	handle
Box 11	shovel	scoop	handle
Box 12	child	face	hands
Box 13	stove	burners	oven
Box 14	sink	faucets	drain
Box 15	airplane	wings	propeller

GROUP INSTRUCTION

To play **Flip Your Lid**, Game I:

1. Seat the children in a circle around the closed boxes.
2. Follow these steps with each box.

Flip Your Lid

- Name the parts as the pictures are shown.
- Ask a child to guess the whole.
- Open box to check.
- Name the whole correctly.

3. Give children turns to follow the same steps with each box.

To play **Flip Your Lid,** Game II:

Place six closed boxes around the spinner. Place the extra closed boxes close by.

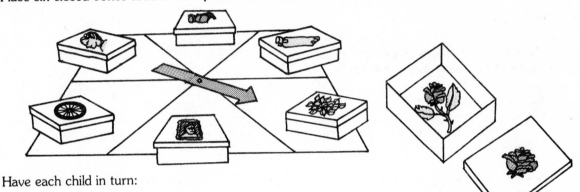

Have each child in turn:

1. Spin the spinner.
2. Look at the top and the bottom of the box selected by the spinner, name the pictures, and try to decide what picture is inside.
3. Name the picture he thinks will be inside.
4. Open the box to check.
5. If answer is correct, retain the box and replace it with a different box on the spinner, until all extra boxes are used.
6. If answer is incorrect, return the box to the spinner.

End the game by asking each child to count his boxes.

INDEPENDENT LEARNING CENTER

To play **Flip Your Lid,** Task I:

Put out all the open boxes with inside of tops and outside of bottoms visible (one part and the whole).

Have the child:

1. Find a part related to each whole.
2. Check by looking inside bottom. (Correct choices will show matching pictures inside the box.)
3. Close the box when a correct match is made.
4. Continue until all boxes are closed.

Flip Your Lid

To play **Flip Your Lid,** Task II:

Repeat with inside of bottoms and outside of tops visible (the other part and the whole).

To play **Flip Your Lid,** Task III:

Repeat with outsides visible (parts only).

MEETING INDIVIDUAL NEEDS

- Decrease difficulty level of any of these activities by working with a few of the boxes at a time. Gradually increase the number as children become familiar with the vocabulary and relationships.

Film Can Activities

MATERIALS IN COMMON

- 35mm film cans available free from many film processing companies

MAKING MATERIALS

To make film cans into sound cylinders:

1. Make sound cylinders in pairs by putting identical items into two film cans with lids. Suggested contents for ten pairs:

   1. one rubber band
   2. ½ teaspoon rice
   3. one metal thimble
   4. one teaspoon sugar
   5. ball of cotton
   6. one rubber eraser
   7. one staple
   8. pumpkin seeds
   9. one tablespoon of water
   10. one marble covered with water

2. Mark one cylinder in each pair with an X.

3. Mark each pair on the bottom with a different color for self-correction.

Helpful hints

- If you wish to vary the contents of the sound cylinders, be sure to test your ideas. Many different items make very similar sounds when used in sound cylinders. Contents suggested above were chosen because they produce distinctly different sounds.
- Be sure to try the water sounds — they delight children!

Film Can
Activities

To make film cans into smell cylinders:

1. Put items into film cans as specified by activity.
2. Cover with cotton ball.
3. Label contents on bottom of each can.
4. Label contents on lid of each can.

Helpful hints

- Use smell cylinders *without* lids; return lids promptly after use.
- Attach labels to prevent mixing lids and cans, since mixing lids will mix odors.
- Use nonperishable contents for smell cylinders when possible.
- Natural smells are sometimes too subtle.
- When using liquids such as perfume, syrup, or extract, put a few drops directly onto cotton ball.

To make film cans into weight cylinders:

1. Pack eight film cans full of sand.
2. Leave eight film cans empty.

Shake A Match

FOCUS ON

- matching sounds
- using left-to-right progression
- developing basic language concepts:
    *match, under, row, top, bottom,
    same, different, left, right*

MATERIALS

- 10 pairs of sound cylinders
- organizing boards

To make organizing boards:

Use poster board, marking pen, and clear contact to make organizing boards for 4, 6, 8, and 10 pairs of sound cylinders.

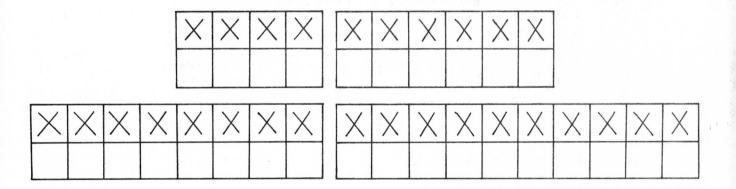

Helpful hints

- Place a green arrow drawn on masking tape or cut from contact paper on the upper left corner of the organizing board to indicate starting point and direction. Remove this cue when no longer needed.

Shake A Match

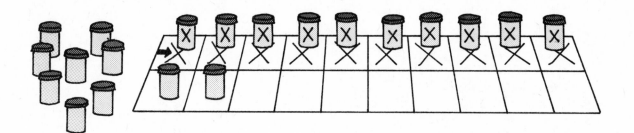

INDEPENDENT LEARNING CENTER

Select one of the organizing boards, based on the child's ability level, and place with the appropriate number of sound cylinders at a learning center. Have the child:

1. Place the X-marked cylinders across the top of the organizing board.
2. Match sounds by

   - Shaking and listening to the X-marked cylinder on the left.
   - Listening to the unmarked cylinders until the same sound is found.
   - Placing this matching cylinder under the corresponding X-marked cylinder on the organizing board.

3. Continue to work from left to right across the board until all sounds are matched.

4. Check his work by lifting each pair of cylinders to see if the color on the bottom is the same.

MEETING INDIVIDUAL NEEDS

- When selecting sound cylinders for the 4, 6, or 8 pair organizing boards, control the level of the task by selecting cylinders requiring more or less difficult sound discriminations.
- If a child insists on using the color-cued cylinder bottoms as a way to match pairs, indicating the sound matching task may be too difficult for him, try modifying the task by using a smaller organizing board and/or cylinders with less similar sounds.

Spin and Match

FOCUS ON

- matching sounds
- remembering things seen and heard
- recognizing and naming: colors, shapes, numerals, letters
- developing basic language concepts:
  same, different, alike, match, pair

MATERIALS

- nine pairs of sound cylinders
- three organizing boards
- double-arrow spinner
- game board

To make organizing boards: Use poster board, marking pen and clear contact to make three organizing boards structured for three pairs each.

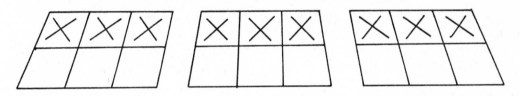

To make double-arrow spinner and game board, design spinner and game board for:

1. Color Identification

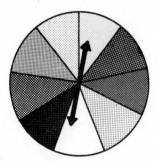

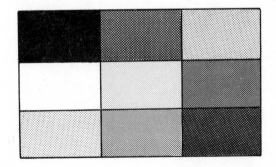

Spin and Match

2. Shape Identification

 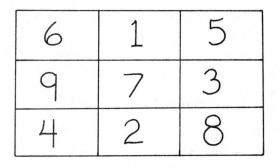

3. Number Identification

 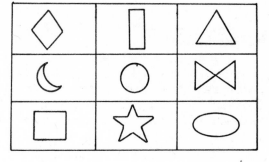

4. Letter Identification

 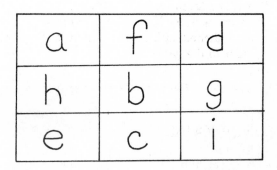

Helpful hints

- Adapt directions for the open-ended spinner in Appendix B for construction of the **Spin and Match** spinner.
- To make a nine-section spinner, begin by dividing circle into thirds.
- Leave game board and spinner blank and cover with clear contact to allow for flexible programming as needed. Use grease pencil or water color felt-tip markers to add colors, shapes, numbers, or letters; old material can be erased and new material added with ease.

Spin and Match

- Remember that the open-ended game board and spinner, as described above, are particularly appropriate for use with letter identification since the full alphabet will not fit on a single board or spinner.

GROUP INSTRUCTION

1. Prepare one game board and one spinner. Instructions are for the Color Identification game. Two or three children may play.
2. Give each child an organizing board, with three X-marked sound cylinders.
3. Ask each child to listen to his sound cylinders and place them on his board.

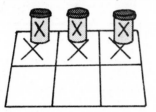

4. Ask the children to listen as you shake each unmarked cylinder and place it on a game board color.

To play **Spin and Match,** have each child in turn:

1. Spin the spinner.
2. Name the two colors as indicated by the double arrow.
3. Find the same two colors on the game board.
4. Choose *one* of the sound cylinders from these two game board colors.
5. Shake and listen to the cylinder.
6. Compare with his X-marked cylinders.
7. Place matched cylinder on his organizing board, or return unmatched cylinder to the game board.

Play continues until organizing boards are filled.

MEETING INDIVIDUAL NEEDS

- Remember, children initially will play this game by trial and error. Some will discover the value of remembering sounds. For others, a reminder will be helpful.

Do You Remember?

FOCUS ON

- matching sounds
- remembering things heard
- developing basic language concepts:
  same, different, alike, match, pair

MATERIALS

- nine pairs of sound cylinders
- game board

To make game board:

1. Divide 12" x 18" poster board into nine sections.
2. Put one picture in each section and cover with clear contact.

Helpful hints

- Vary the pictures on the game board to correlate with units such as:

farm animals	food	community workers
zoo animals	clothing	seasons
pets	transportation	a specific holiday

- Suggested sources of pictures:

magazines	gift wrapping paper
old workbooks	commercial sets of gummed seals
discarded textbooks	mail order catalogs
greeting cards	junk mail
picture stickers, see Appendix C.	

Do You Remember?

GROUP INSTRUCTION

1. Seat a group of up to nine children around the game board.
2. Name the pictures on the game board.
3. Tell the children they will play a listening and remembering game. Say, "I'm going to put one cylinder on each picture. Listen carefully and remember where I put each sound."
4. Shake each X-marked cylinder, and place it on a game board picture. Say, "Now the remembering fun begins!" Have each child in turn:

   1. Choose an unmarked cylinder.
   2. Shake and listen to the sound of this cylinder.
   3. Retain this cylinder.

Next, have each child in turn:

   1. Choose from the game board the sound he remembers as a match for his sound.
   2. Name the game board picture.
   3. Compare the sounds of the cylinders.
   4. Retain a matched pair, or return a cylinder which does not match his to the same picture on the game board.

Continue until each child has found a match for his cylinder.

MEETING INDIVIDUAL NEEDS

- Because the game becomes easier as the number of cylinders to choose from decreases, begin the game with the most capable children to build in better success opportunity for children you predict will have difficulty.
- Since remembering the sounds is hard work, stop and re-listen to the game board cylinder sounds part way through the game. Allow a child to re-listen to his cylinder if he wishes.

Smell a Match

FOCUS ON

- matching smells
- using left to right progression
- developing basic language concepts:
  match, under, row, top, bottom, same, different, left, right

MATERIALS

- 6 pairs of smell cylinders
- 6-pair organizing board as for **Shake a Match**

To make smell cylinders:

1. Choose from these suggested contents:

   six distinctly different perfume or cologne smells
   six distinctly different herb or spice smells
   any combination of these to make six smells

2. Mark one cylinder in each pair with an X.
3. Mark each pair on the bottom with a different color to provide for self-correction.

INDEPENDENT LEARNING CENTER

Place the 12 smell cylinders beside the organizing board at a learning center. Have the child:

1. Place the X-marked smell cylinders across the top of the organizing board.
2. Smell the X-marked cylinder on the left.
3. Smell the unmarked cylinders to find a match.
4. Place the matching cylinder under the corresponding X-marked cylinder on the organizing board.

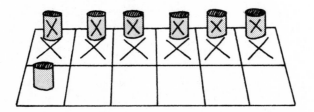

5. Continue from left to right across the board until all smells are matched.
6. Check by lifting each pair of cylinders to see if the color on the bottom is the same.

Smell a Match

MEETING INDIVIDUAL NEEDS

- Alter the difficulty of the task by increasing or decreasing the number of smell cylinder pairs.
- If a child insists on using the color-cued cylinder bottoms as a way to match pairs, provide less difficult tasks for him.

Smelly Things

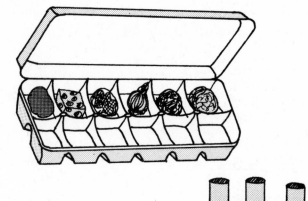

FOCUS ON

- recognizing smells
- relating smells to objects
- developing basic language concepts:
    match, under, row, top, bottom

MATERIALS

- 6 smell cylinders
- egg carton

Contents of smell cylinders:
1. a few drops of coconut extract or flavoring
2. fresh coffee grounds
3. Parmesan cheese
4. peanut butter
5. dried onion flakes
6. whole cloves

To prepare egg carton, wrap these items in clear plastic, and place them in the top row of the carton:

1. shredded coconut
2. fresh coffee grounds
3. chunk of hard cheese
4. peanuts
5. small dry onion
6. whole cloves

INDEPENDENT LEARNING CENTER

Help the child name the contents of the egg carton. Have the child:

1. Match a smell to an object.
2. Place the smell cylinder in the bottom row of the egg carton under the object.
3. Continue until all smells are matched to objects.

Banana, Apple, or Nuts?

FOCUS ON

- recognizing smells
- relating smells to pictures
- developing basic language concepts:
  match

MATERIALS

- smell cylinders
- picture cards

Contents of smell cylinders:

1. imitation strawberry extract
2. instant chocolate for milk
3. maple syrup
4. mint extract
5. peanut butter
6. Max Factor Green Apple Perfume Oil
7. banana extract
8. lemon extract
9. dried onion flakes
10. orange extract

Prepare one picture card for each:

1. strawberry ice cream cone
2. chocolate milk
3. pancakes with syrup
4. gum
5. nuts
6. apple
7. banana
8. lemon
9. onion
10. orange

Helpful hint

- If the Peabody Language Development Kit, Level P, is available, use these cards: f 14, f 17, f 20, f 32, f 37, f 38, f 39, f 42, f 43, f 44.

INDEPENDENT LEARNING CENTER

Ask the child to name the pictures. Have the child:

1. Match a smell to the corresponding food picture.
2. Place the smell cylinder on the picture.
3. Continue until all smells and pictures are matched.

MEETING INDIVIDUAL NEEDS

- Begin this activity with as few as two smell cylinders and corresponding pictures. Increase the number gradually to assure success for children having difficulty.

Smell and Think Lotto

FOCUS ON

- recognizing and naming smells
- relating two objects

MATERIALS

- 8 smell cylinders
- lotto board

Contents of smell cylinders:
1. pine needles
2. toothpaste
3. Baco-bits
4. perfume
5. turpentine
6. sardine oil
7. gasoline
8. bleach

To make lotto board: Use 12″ x 16″ poster board, marking pen, clear contact, and these pictures from Appendix A-7:

1. Christmas package
2. toothbrush
3. egg
4. glamorous lady
5. paint brush
6. fishing pole
7. car
8. laundry on a clothesline

Smell and Think Lotto

GROUP INSTRUCTION

Identify and discuss pictures on the lotto board.

To play **Smell and Think Lotto,** have each child in turn:

1. Choose a smell cylinder, and decide which picture could go with the smell — but he must not tell!
2. Pass the cylinder quickly from child to child until each of the other children has a turn to smell and think.
3. When the cylinder returns to the original child, smell again and place the cylinder on one of the lotto board pictures.
4. Ask the other children if he chose the correct picture.

Continue the game until all the cans are on the board.

INDEPENDENT LEARNING CENTER

After the children are familiar with this game, allow them to play it individually at a learning center.

Which Weigh?

FOCUS ON

- using tactile-kinesthetic information
- recognizing weight differences
- developing basic language concepts:
  heavy, light, bottom, match

MATERIALS

- 16 film can weight cylinders
- two response boards

To prepare weight cylinders:

Use a black marking pen to draw a leaf on the bottom of each of eight empty film cans, and a car on the bottom of each of eight full film cans.

To prepare response boards:

Draw a car and a leaf on 9" x 12" tagboard or poster board and cover with contact. Cut out car and leaf.

INDEPENDENT LEARNING CENTER

Set up the weight cylinders with response boards at a learning center. Have the child:

1. Sort the weight cylinders, putting all the heavy cylinders on the car board and all the light cylinders on the leaf board.

2. Check by turning the cylinders over. The picture on the bottom of each cylinder should match the response board on which it was placed.

Hat Activities

MATERIALS IN COMMON

- assorted hats

FINDING MATERIALS

- Ask parents of students, other teachers, your own family, and friends to save interesting hats for you.

BUYING MATERIALS

- Excellent sources for inexpensive hats:

    - Goodwill, Salvation Army, or other used clothing stores
    - rummage sales
    - garage sales
    - flea markets

Hat Shop

FOCUS ON

- recognizing and naming colors
- recognizing and naming numerals
- counting
- naming common materials
- relating part to whole
- understanding and using descriptive language
- developing basic language concepts:
    light, dark, wide, narrow, big, little, large,
    small, medium-sized, top, around, side, front, back,
    several, few, many, with, without, least, most, next

MATERIALS

- assorted hats
- play money — dollar bills
- mirror

To prepare hats:

Assign a price of $1 to $6 to each hat. Attach a price tag. Use convenient self-stick labels or masking tape for this purpose.

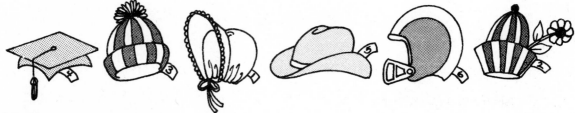

GROUP INSTRUCTION

To play **Hat Shop,** Game I (Understanding Descriptive Language):

Set up the Hat Shop with hats and a mirror.

1. Say, "We're going to pretend this is a Hat Shop. Listen carefully — I'll tell you about the hat I'm thinking of buying. I'm thinking of buying a hat . . . (tell one thing about the hat)."
2. Call on a child to choose the hat.
3. If the choice is not correct, continue, "I'm thinking of a hat . . . (repeat the first description, and add *one* more description)."
4. Call on a different child.
5. Continue adding one description at a time until the correct hat is chosen.
6. When a correct choice is made, give the hat to the child to wear.
7. If a child is already wearing a hat when he makes a correct choice, allow him to decide whether to trade hats.

Hat Shop

Describe hats in terms of:

- label — helmet, stocking cap, sun hat
- color — light, dark, color names
- size — big, little, large, small, medium-sized
- cost — $1, $5, more than, less than, least, most, enough
- condition — old, new, dirty, clean
- material — felt, straw, plastic, wool, rubber, net
- parts — crown, bill, brim, band, strap, buckle
- trim — flowers, veil, ribbon, feathers, tassel, fur
- position of trim — top, around, front, back, side
- quantity of trim — several, few, many
- function — safety (to ride on a motorcycle)
    - warmth (to ski)
    - protection (to take a shower)
    - beauty (to go to church)
    - humor (to work at the circus)

To play **Hat Shop,** Game II (Using Descriptive Language):

Set up the Hat Shop with hats and a mirror. Call on a child to tell about a hat he is thinking of buying. Continue as for Game I, changing children each time a correct hat is chosen.

INDIVIDUAL INSTRUCTION

For another game focusing on use of descriptive language, have each child in turn:

1. Go "shopping" in the Hat Shop.
2. Choose one hat to buy.
3. Tell about this hat in as many different ways as possible.
4. Receive one play money dollar for each different description.
5. "Buy" the hat when he has enough dollars.
6. Put the hat on, and look in the mirror.
7. Wear the hat.

INDEPENDENT LEARNING CENTER

When children have learned to use the descriptive language required for **Hat Shop,** set up the Hat Shop with a child as shopkeeper. Have the other children take turns buying hats, as in **Hat Shop,** Individual Instruction.

Hat Shop

MEETING INDIVIDUAL NEEDS

- When playing the **Hat Shop** group games, remember to call on a child *after* a description is given. This strategy helps maintain the attention of each child to each description.
- When playing the **Hat Shop** group games, be aware that a child is likely to choose a hat which fits the description but is not correct. This is particularly true after the first description. When this happens, help the child understand that the description fits more than one hat. Say something like, "That's a *good* choice! That hat does have a wide brim, but I'm thinking of another hat with a wide brim."
- Before playing group Game II, play Game I several times in order to model the descriptive language and specific basic concepts to be emphasized.
- When playing group Game II, begin with those children who have the best verbal skills. Their descriptions will provide another model for the group.
- When a child gives a description that is not a sentence, model this description in a full sentence.

If child says:	Teacher models:
"helmet"	"This is a helmet."
"blue"	"This hat is blue."
"funny hat"	"The clown hat is funny."

- If a child has difficulty with the descriptive language task in Hat Shop, Individual Instruction, try RESPONSE STRUCTURING providing gradually increasing amounts of assistance until a successful response is achieved. The RESPONSE STRUCTURING technique is described in the mitten and glove activity **How Many Ways?**

1. Focus attention on a specific attribute, for example:

   "What material is this hat made of?"

2. Provide necessary information in the form of a multiple choice question, for example:

   "Is this hat made of straw, felt, or plastic?"

3. Provide necessary information in the form of a yes-no question, for example:

   "Is this hat made of straw?"

4. Provide a complete model for response and ask the child to imitate, for example:

   "Say after me: This hat is made of straw."

Hat Shop

Reinforce the correct response immediately with praise!

- When playing **Hat Shop,** Individual Instruction, raise prices as the children increase their descriptive language skills.

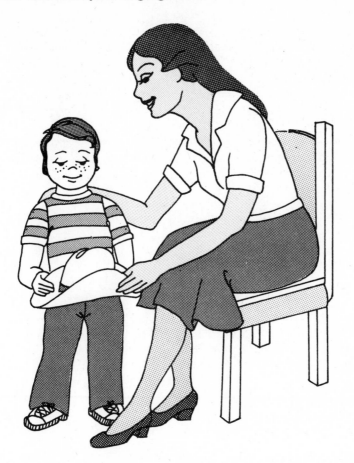

Look At Me

FOCUS ON

- recognizing sounds
- relating sounds to people and places
- role playing
- developing basic language concepts:
  next, last, none

MATERIALS

- assortment of hats
- teacher-made cassette tape
- mirror

To select hat assortment

For this game, select hats that can be related to environmental sounds. Some suggestions:

hat	related sound
baby bonnet	baby cooing and/or crying
firefighter's hat	fire siren
cowhand's hat	horse galloping and/or neighing
hard hat	construction sounds such as jackhammer
bathing cap	children splashing and playing in a swimming pool
football helmet	sports announcer at a football game
motorcycle helmet	motorcycle engine
bride's veil	organ wedding music
rain hat	rain and thunder
stocking cap	wintry wind
clown hat	circus sounds
baseball cap	umpire calling strikes
sailor's cap	fog horn
pilot's cap	airplane flying
graduation cap (mortar board)	voice saying, "This diploma is for Raymond Montoya," followed by applause
nurse's cap	voice saying, "Your temperature is normal. Do you feel better now?"

To prepare teacher-made cassette tape:

Collect sounds which can be obtained from the following sources:

direct environmental sounds
commercially programmed material on record or tape
sound effects libraries at local radio stations

Look At Me

When you have collected the sounds on various tapes and records, prepare a cassette.

1. Record, "This is a listening game with hats and sounds. Listen carefully to each sound. Find the hat that goes with the sound. Put on the hat, and use the mirror to see how you look. Are you ready? Now find the hat that goes with this sound."
2. Record a sound taken from tape or record — for example, the sound of a fire engine. (Duration of sound should allow sufficient time for the child to find the hat, put it on, and look in the mirror.)
3. Record, "Did you know that was a fire engine? Good! Take off the firefighter's hat and be ready to listen for the next sound."
4. Repeat steps two and three for each different hat-sound combination.
5. End the tape by recording, "Take off the _____ hat. That was the *last* sound."

Helpful hints

- If you have a child whose parents enjoy projects involving tapes and recording, ask them to prepare a tape for the class.
- Remember, a bride's veil has special appeal for little girls. Though it may be hard to find through second-hand sources, make one easily using a white head band, white artificial flowers, and white net. Gather the net and attach to the head band. Add a finishing touch with the white flowers.

GROUP INSTRUCTION

1. Seat the children around the assortment of hats.
2. Identify and discuss each of the hats with the children.
3. Tell the children, "We're going to play a *listening* game. *None* of us will talk. The tape will tell you what to do. When I hand you the mirror, you'll know it's your turn."
4. Turn on the tape.
5. Use the mirror to signal turns as the children follow instructions on the tape.

INDEPENDENT LEARNING CENTER

Set up the hats and tape player where each child can have a turn to follow all the taped instructions independently.

MEETING INDIVIDUAL NEEDS

- While both boys and girls usually enjoy trying on all the hats, occasionally a child may be embarrassed by wearing a particular hat. Allow this child to simply indicate the correct hat without putting it on.

Ellie and Elmer Emptyhead

FOCUS ON

- differentiating between singular and plural
- answering and asking "wh" questions
- developing basic language concepts:
  inside, empty, after, early, late, never, always

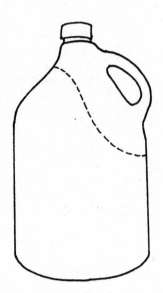

MATERIALS

- assorted hats
- Ellie and Elmer Emptyhead

To make Ellie and Elmer:

1. Remove labels from two plastic one gallon bleach jugs.
2. Cut the spouts and handles off.
3. Turn jugs upside down.
4. Draw features for Ellie.
5. Draw features and a beard for Elmer.
6. Use two unopened 46 ounce juice cans as stands to provide stability for Ellie and Elmer.

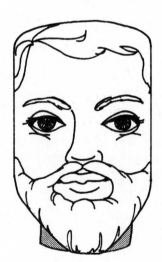

Ellie and Elmer Emptyhead

GROUP INSTRUCTION

Introduce the children to Ellie and Elmer Emptyhead. Show the children that Ellie and Elmer have heads that are empty inside. Tell the children that Ellie and Elmer have no brains, so they will need to help to think!

To play **Ellie and Elmer Emptyhead,** Game I (Answering *Who* Questions):

1. Put a hat(s) on Ellie and/or Elmer.
2. Ask, "Who is wearing a hat?"
3. Provide assistance, as needed, until children can answer correctly:

> "Elmer is wearing a hat."
> "Ellie is wearing a hat."
> "Ellie and Elmer are wearing hats."

To play **Ellie and Elmer Emptyhead,** Game II (Answering *Where* Questions):

1. Put a hat(s) on Ellie and/or Elmer.
2. Ask, "Where could Ellie and/or Elmer wear this/these hat(s)?"
3. Provide assistance, as needed, until children can give answers such as:

> "Elmer could wear that hat on a ski slope."
> "Ellie could wear that hat to a shopping center."
> "Elmer and Ellie could wear those hats to church."

To play **Ellie and Elmer Emptyhead,** Game III (Answering *When* Questions):

1. Put a hat(s) on Ellie and/or Elmer.
2. Ask, "When could/should Ellie and/or Elmer wear this/these hat(s)?"
3. Provide assistance, as needed, until children can give answers such as:

> "Elmer could wear that hat in the wintertime."
> "Ellie could wear that hat after putting curlers in her hair."
> "Ellie could wear that hat on a rainy day."
> "Elmer could wear that hat early in the morning."
> "Ellie could wear that hat late at night."
> "Ellie and Elmer should never wear those hats on a hot day."
> "Elmer should always wear that hat when he rides on a motorcycle."

To play **Ellie and Elmer Emptyhead,** Game IV (Answering *Why* Questions):

1. Put a hat(s) on Ellie and/or Elmer.
2. Ask, "Why would Ellie and/or Elmer wear this/these hat(s)?"
3. Provide assistance, as needed, until children can give answers such as:

> "Ellie would wear that hat to keep warm."
> "Ellie and Elmer would wear those hats so they don't get sunburned."

Ellie and Elmer Emptyhead

"Ellie would wear that hat to look pretty."
"Elmer would wear that hat to look handsome."
"Ellie would wear that hat to keep her hair dry."
"Elmer would wear that helmet so he doesn't get hurt."

To play **Ellie and Elmer Emptyhead,** Game V (Answering *What* Questions):

1. Put a hat(s) on Ellie and/or Elmer.
2. Ask, "What could Ellie and/or Elmer do wearing this/these hat(s)?"
3. Provide assistance, as needed, until children can give answers such as:

   "Ellie could work in the garden."
   "Elmer could play football."
   "Ellie and Elmer could walk in the rain."
   "Ellie could eat lunch with a friend."
   "Elmer could travel on an airplane."

To play **Ellie and Elmer Emptyhead,** Game VI (Answering *Who, Where, When, Why, What* Questions):

1. Allow one child at a time to choose a hat and put it on.
2. Ask the remainder of the children assorted who, where, when, why, what questions about this hat.

To play **Ellie and Elmer Emptyhead,** Game VII (Asking *Who, Where, When, Why, What* Questions):

1. Allow one child at a time to choose a hat and put it on.
2. Have the remainder of the children, one at a time, ask each other who, where, when, why, what questions about this hat.

Ellie and Elmer Emptyhead

MEETING INDIVIDUAL NEEDS

- Remember, some groups of children will need to spend an entire lesson(s) on each of the Games I through VII; other groups of children will be able to play two or more games in a single lesson. Move from one game to the next as children master the skills.
- To provide assistance in all of these games, restructure the "wh" questions for children who are unable to respond successfully. Restructure these questions so that all the necessary information is provided. Require choices and judgments from the child, but not original ideas. This is an example of the use of the RESPONSE STRUCTURING technique as described in the mitten and glove activity **How Many Ways?**

MULTIPLE CHOICE QUESTIONS

"Would Elmer wear this hat to go to a party, to go for a picnic on the beach, or to play football?"

"Would Ellie wear this hat in the wintertime or in the summertime?"

YES-NO QUESTIONS

"Would Elmer wear this hat to ride a motorcycle?"

"Would Ellie wear this cap in a swimming pool?"

If the response is not in a complete sentence, model the sentence and ask the child to repeat it. "Yes, Ellie would wear this cap to a swimming pool." Move the child back to the "wh" question, "*Good*, now tell me: *Where* would Ellie wear this cap?"

- Be very careful about rejecting children's ideas in this game. Ask a child to explain material which seems illogical. For example: "Elmer could wear the football helmet in a store." Explanation: "My Daddy wore his helmet in a store where they took his picture."

Ellie and Elmer at Work

FOCUS ON

- expanding traditional sex roles
- using pronouns correctly
- relating hats to occupations

MATERIALS

- hats related to occupations
- Ellie and Elmer (See **Ellie and Elmer Emptyhead**)

To select hats, include any of these which are available. Where possible, include two hats for each occupation.

firefighter's hat	engineer's cap	pilot's hat
cowhand's hat	clown's hat	surgical nurse's cap
hard hat	baseball cap	police uniform hat
football helmet	sailor's hat	farmer's straw hat

Helpful hint

- Ask if mothers and fathers wear special hats for work. Parents may be able to add to your collection, and your instructions can include local information such as, "They work at the XYZ Drive-In."

GROUP INSTRUCTION

1. Seat the children in front of Ellie and Elmer with the hat assortment nearby.
2. Discuss the hats and the occupations with which they are associated. Continue to step 3 only after children have learned to name the hats.
3. Say, "Let's see how Ellie and Elmer would look in some of these jobs. Listen carefully and give them the correct hats . . .
    She is a firefighter.
    He is a football player.
    He is a nurse.
    She is a cowhand.
    They are sailors.
    She is a construction worker.
    He is a clown.
    They are farmers.
    They are baseball players."

4. After each statement, call on one child to give Ellie and/or Elmer appropriate hats. The statements suggested are examples only. Use statements based on available hats. Remember that you must have two hats for an occupation to give a "they" instruction.

MEETING INDIVIDUAL NEEDS

- Be sure to choose the child who is to respond *after* the statement is made. This strategy will help maintain the attention of each child to each statement.

Thumbtack Activities

MATERIALS IN COMMON

- thumbtacks or pushpins in assorted colors
- tack boards
- spirit master task pages

BUYING MATERIALS

- Purchase thumbtacks and pushpins in assorted colors at discount stores, dime stores, or drugstores.

MAKING MATERIALS

To make tack boards:

Cut 9″ x 12″ piece of cork, insulation board, ceiling tile, or corrugated cardboard. Tack boards must be at least ¼″ thick for thumbtacks and ½″ thick for pushpins. To finish and protect the edges, bind them with plastic tape or cloth tape.

To prepare spirit master task pages:

Put selected content on an 8½″ x 11″ spirit master, and run off enough copies for each child to have his own page. Appendix A-8 contains several **Tack-It** pages intended for reproduction; those not provided in the appendix should be drawn directly on a spirit master sheet and reproduced.

HELPFUL HINTS

- Glue thin cork to corrugated cardboard to make a tack board that is both durable and inexpensive. Thin cork squares are available with self-stick backing.
- Some tack board materials hold tacks more firmly than others. Children should be able to remove their own tacks when their tasks are completed.
- Consider acquiring a Thumbtack Puller for your children's enjoyment (see Appendix C).
- Use a bulletin board as the tack board for **Tack-It** activities when setting up a bulletin board learning center.

Tack-It

FOCUS ON

- developing manipulative skills
- recognizing colors
- other skills as specified for each **Tack-It** page
- developing basic language concepts:
    concepts as specified for each **Tack-It** page

MATERIALS

- thumbtacks or pushpins in assorted colors
- tack boards
- spirit master task pages
- crayons

Helpful hints

- To set up **Tack-It** pages, place selected spirit master task page on tack board and provide thumbtacks or pushpins.
- Once an activity is completed, the perforated task page makes a take-home reward for task completion.
- Do not limit yourself to the designs for tasks illustrated here. Use your creativity!

GROUP INSTRUCTION

Use **Tack-It** pages with a small group to monitor the responses of several children at once.

Tack-It

INDIVIDUAL INSTRUCTION

Use Tack-It pages individually if a child has unusual difficulty with the activity. Tack-It pages are excellent for use by an aide or volunteer for individualized instruction.

INDEPENDENT LEARNING CENTER

Set out most Tack-It pages for independent work at a center after giving verbal instructions to emphasize the language concepts involved. Monitor the children's work adequately to prevent the practice of error.

MEETING INDIVIDUAL NEEDS

- Because of the detailed nature of the manipulative and near-point visual tasks required, keep each Tack-It activity short. While some children will be able to work with these materials longer than others, all children will benefit most from short work times followed by activities focused on very different skills.
- In order to develop basic language concepts, remember that children need to verbalize concepts as well as hear them. When you ask a child to repeat instructions, you provide an opportunity for him to practice using the language concepts verbally.
- If a child has difficulty, simplify the task by breaking it down into steps. For example, Task 2 for **Tack-It #3** is:

  Begin at the left.
  Put a row of blue tacks on the middle line.

To simplify this, follow these steps:

1. Say, "Find a blue tack." Assist, if necessary, by guiding the child's hand to a blue tack. *Reinforce this correct response with praise!*
2. Say, "Find the left side of the page." Assist and reinforce, as above.
3. Say, "Find the line in the middle." Assist and reinforce, as above.
4. Say, "Begin at the left. Put the blue tack on the middle line." Assist and reinforce, as above.
5. Ask, "What color is the tack?"
   "Where did you begin?"
   "Which line did you put the tack on?"
   If child offers one word answers, model a complete sentence, "Good, the tack is blue."

6. Continue to assist the child until he is able to work independently.

- Vary the colors of tacks used according to the color concepts being emphasized.
- When choosing between thumbtacks and pushpins, consider the developmental levels of the individual children. Pushpins require controlled use of a two- or three-finger pincer grasp. Thumbtacks involve more control because they require

Tack-It

a three-finger pincer grasp coordinated with a release-push. Some children who cannot do the manipulative parts of these tasks with thumbtacks can be successful with pushpins.

- For the child who needs bilateral activities, use pushpins since they can be removed from the tack board with both hands simultaneously.
- If Tack-It activities are used at a bulletin board learning center, be aware that the use of thumbtacks on a vertical surface presents an even more difficult manipulative task. Children who are not successful should be allowed to return to a horizontal surface or change from thumbtacks to pushpins.
- Remember, these activities are obviously inappropriate for very immature children who tend to mouth materials; in the experience of these authors, however, this was rarely a problem. Children enjoy being trusted with "adult" materials, such as thumbtacks, and usually respond by living up to that trust.

TACK-IT #1

FOCUS ON

- using left-to-right progression
- developing basic language concepts:
    row, between, line, left, begin

Have the child:

Begin at the left.
Put a row of green tacks between the two lines.

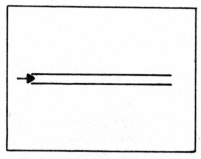

Draw the above on an 8½ x 11 spirit master sheet, and reproduce one copy for each child.

Tack-It

TACK-IT #2

FOCUS ON

- using left to right progression
- developing basic language concepts:
  over, under, row, line, left, begin

Have the child:

Task 1. Put yellow tacks over the line.

Task 2. Put red tacks under the line.

Task 3. Begin at the left.
Put a row of green tacks on the line.

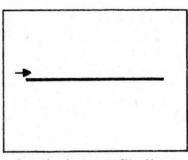

Draw the above on an 8½ x 11
spirit master sheet, and
reproduce one copy for each child.

TACK-IT #3

FOCUS ON

- using left to right progression
- developing basic language concepts:
  top, middle, bottom, row, between, line, left, begin

Have the child:

Task 1. Begin at the left.
Put a row of red tacks on the top line.

Task 2. Begin at the left.
Put a row of blue tacks on the middle line.

Task 3. Begin at the left.
Put a row of yellow tacks on the bottom line.

Task 4. Put green tacks between the top line and the middle line.

Task 5. Put blue tacks between the middle line and the bottom line.

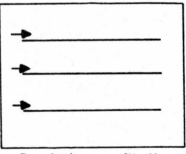

Draw the above on an 8½ x 11
spirit master sheet, and
reproduce one copy for each child.

Tack-It

TACK-IT #4

FOCUS ON

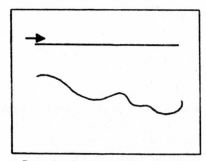

- using left-to-right progression
- developing basic language concepts:
  row, straight, curved, line, left, begin

Have the child:

Task 1. Begin at the left.
Put a row of blue tacks on the straight line.

Task 2. Begin at the left.
Put red tacks on the curved line.

Draw the above on an 8½ x 11 spirit master sheet, and reproduce one copy for each child.

TACK-IT #5

FOCUS ON

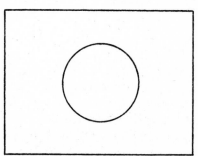

- developing basic language concepts:
  around, outside, inside

Have the child:

Task 1. Put yellow tacks around the outside of the circle.

Task 2. Put green tacks around the inside of the circle.

Draw the above on an 8½ x 11 spirit master sheet, and reproduce one copy for each child.

134

Tack-It

TACK-IT #6

FOCUS ON

- recognizing shapes
- developing basic language concepts: *inside, outside*

Have the child:

Task 1. Trace the square with a finger.
Put yellow tacks on the square.

Task 2. Put red tacks inside the square.

Task 3. Put blue tacks outside the square.

Draw the above
on an 8½ x 11 spirit
master sheet, and
reproduce one copy
for each child.

Repeat for other shapes. A spirit master task page can be made for any shape.

TACK-IT #7

FOCUS ON

- recognizing and naming shapes
- counting
- developing basic language concepts:
  corner, every, with, least, most

Have the child:

Task 1. Find and name all the shapes with corners.
Put a blue tack on every corner.

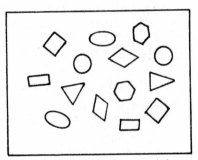

We've prepared the above worksheet for you. See Appendix A-8.

Task 2. Count the corners on one square.
Tell how many corners a square has.
Find and name other shapes with as many corners as a square.
Put green tacks on the corners of these shapes.

Task 3. Find and name the shape with the least corners.
Count the corners.
Put red tacks on these corners.

Task 4. Find and name the shape with the most corners.
Count the corners.
Put yellow tacks on these corners.

Tack-It

TACK-IT #8

FOCUS ON

- recognizing shapes
- developing basic language concepts:
  center, every, little, medium-sized, big, small, large

Have the child:

We've prepared the above worksheet for you. See Appendix A-9.

Task 1. Find all the little (or small) squares.
Put a green tack in the center of every little square.

Task 2. Find all the medium-sized squares.
Put a blue tack in the center of every medium-sized square.

Task 3. Find all the big (or large) squares.
Put a red tack in the center of every big square.

Repeat for triangles. Other spirit master pages can be made with any combination of shapes and sizes.

TACK-IT #9

FOCUS ON

- using tactile-kinesthetic information
- counting
- recognizing numerals
- relating numerals to quantity
- developing basic language concepts:
  line, under

Draw the above on an 8½ x 11 spirit master sheet, and reproduce one copy for each child.

Have the child:

Count 5 blue tacks and put them on the line under the 5.
Trace the 5 with his finger.
Put blue tacks on the 5.

Repeat for other numerals. A spirit master page can be made for any numeral.

Tack-It

TACK-IT #10

FOCUS ON

- recognizing numerals
- developing basic language concepts:
  under, below, over, above, every

Have the child:

Task 1. Put a yellow tack under (or below) every 5.

Task 2. Put a green tack over (or above) every 8.

Repeat for other numerals.

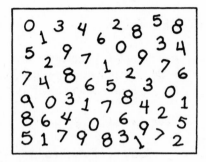

Draw the above on an 8½ x 11
spirit master sheet, and reproduce
one copy for each child.

TACK-IT #11

FOCUS ON

- using tactile-kinesthetic information
- recognizing letters

Have the child:

Trace the letter with his finger.
Put green tacks on the letter.

Repeat for other letters. A spirit master page can be made for any letter, small
or capital.

Draw the above on an 8½ x 11 spirit
master sheet, and reproduce one copy
for each child.

Tack-It

TACK-IT #12

FOCUS ON

- differentiating between letters and numerals
- developing basic language concepts:
  under, below, over, above, every

Have the child:

Task 1. Put a red tack under (or below) every letter.

Task 2. Put a yellow tack over (or above) every numeral.

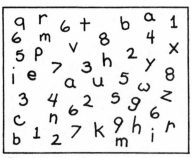

Draw the above on an 8½ x 11 spirit master sheet, and reproduce one copy for each child.

TACK-IT #13

FOCUS ON

- developing basic language concepts:
  long, short, match

Have the child:

Color the long dress yellow.
Color the short dress green.
Use tacks for buttons.
Make the buttons match the dress.

We've prepared the above worksheet for you. See Appendix A-10.

TACK-IT #14

FOCUS ON

- developing basic language concepts:
  match

Have the child:

Color the cars red or blue.
Use tacks for wheels.
Make the wheels match the cars.

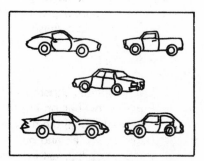

We've prepared the above worksheet for you. See Appendix A-11.

Tack-It

TACK-IT #15

FOCUS ON

- developing basic language concepts:
  center, every

Have the child:

   Put a yellow tack in the center of every flower.

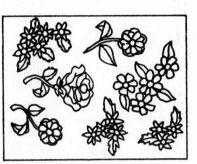

We've prepared the above worksheet for you. See Appendix A-12.

TACK-IT #16

FOCUS ON

- developing basic language concepts
  wide, narrow

Have the child:

   Task 1.   Decorate the wide belts with red tacks.

   Task 2.   Decorate the narrow belts with yellow tacks.

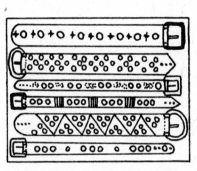

We've prepared the above worksheet for you. See Appendix A-13.

TACK-IT #17

FOCUS ON

- developing basic language concepts:
  *top, middle, every, row, begin,
  left, first, last, finish*

Have the child:

   Use tacks for Christmas balls to decorate the tree.
   Put a yellow ball on the top of the tree.
   Put a red ball in the middle of every row.
   Begin at the left and put a blue ball first in every row.
   Put a green ball last in every row.
   Choose colors to finish decorating the tree.

We've prepared the above worksheet for you. See Appendix A-14.

Tacky Patterns

FOCUS ON

- developing manipulative skills
- recognizing and naming colors
- using left to right progression
- continuing sequential patterns seen
- remembering — in sequence — patterns seen
- remembering — in sequence — patterns heard
- developing basic language concepts:
    begin, line, left, right, top, bottom, next, last, same, different, alike, first, second, third

MATERIALS

- thumbtacks or pushpins in assorted colors
- tack board
- spirit master task page
- piece of cloth

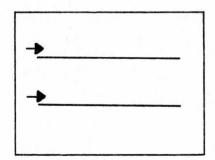

Draw the above on an 8½ x 11 spirit master sheet, and reproduce one copy for each child.

INDIVIDUAL INSTRUCTION

To play **Tacky Patterns,** Game I (Continuing — In sequence — Patterns Seen):

Beginning on the left, arrange thumbtacks (or pushpins) on one line to start a sequential color pattern which the child continues across the task page.

- Color Pattern/Two
    red - yellow - red - yellow - red . . .

- Color Pattern/Three
    blue - blue - green - blue - blue . . .

- Color Pattern/Four
    red - green - green - blue - red - green - green . . .

To play **Tacky Patterns,** Game II (Remembering — In Sequence — Patterns Seen):

1. Beginning on the left, arrange a pattern on the top line of the task page.
2. Allow time for the child to look carefully at the pattern.
3. Cover the pattern with a cloth.
4. Ask the child to make a pattern that is the same on the bottom line.
5. Have the child lift the cloth to check his pattern. If he has made errors, encourage him to use the model on the top line to correct his pattern. This allows each child to finish with a correct response!

Tacky Patterns

To play **Tacky Patterns**, Game III (Continuing — In sequence — Patterns Heard):

1. Turn the tack board so the child *cannot see the task page*.
2. Arrange a pattern on the top line, verbalizing the pattern as you work. Say, "I'll *tell* you what my line looks like. Listen carefully! Red, yellow, red."
3. Cover the pattern with a cloth.
4. Turn the tack board to face the child.
5. Ask the child to make a pattern that is the *same* on the bottom row.
6. Have the child lift the cloth to check his pattern. If he has made errors, encourage him to use the model on the top line to correct his pattern. This allows each child to finish with a correct response!

MEETING INDIVIDUAL NEEDS

- Depending on the child's ability level, begin with a pattern of two, three, or four. Increase the length of the pattern as the child develops skill.
- Control the difficulty level of these tasks by the number of color choices provided for the child. Colors, in addition to those necessary to complete the pattern, serve as distractors, thus making the tasks more challenging.
- To help a child who is unsuccessful, ask him to say the pattern with you or repeat the pattern immediately after he sees or hears it.
- When verbalizing patterns, use your voice as a cue to group. For example, "Red, yellow, (pause), red, yellow."
- For the child who needs bilateral activities, use pushpins since they can be removed from the tack board with both hands simultaneously.
- Vary the language used in presenting these tasks according to the child's level of concept development. Emphasize any of the concepts listed under "developing basic language concepts."

Appendix A-1   Lock-Up
Reproduce and mount pictures on ten 3″ x 5″ cards to make Lock-Up picture cards.

Appendix A-2 Pocket Puzzles
Reproduce and mount pictures on fifteen 3″ x 5″ cards to make Pocket Puzzle cue cards.

144

145

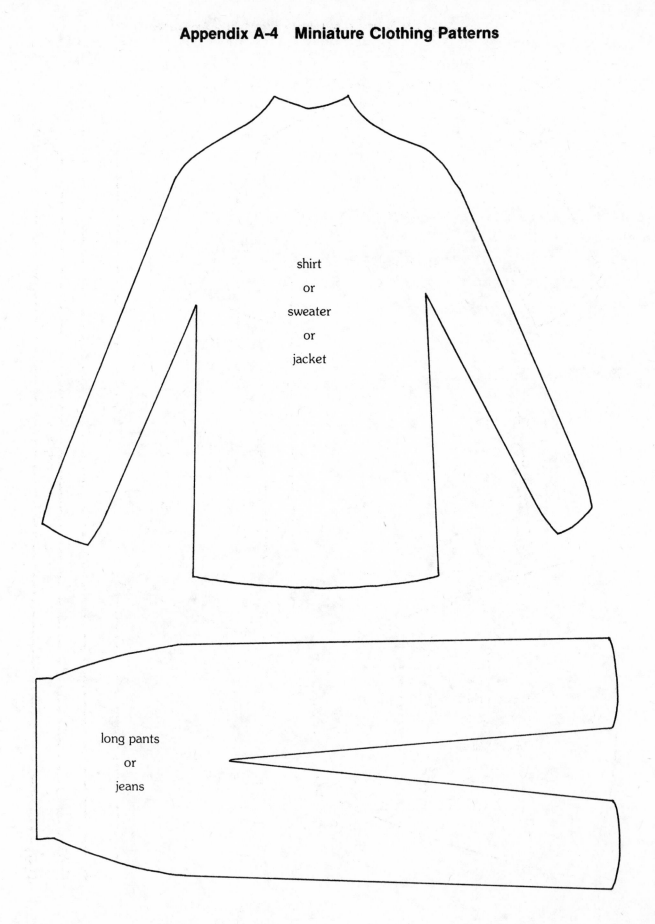

shirt
or
sweater
or
jacket

long pants
or
jeans

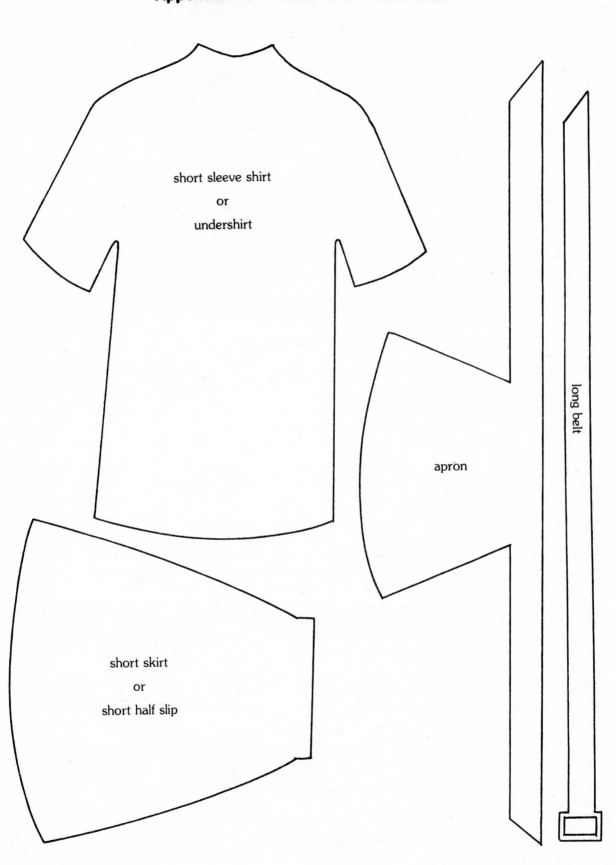

short sleeve shirt
or
undershirt

apron

long belt

short skirt
or
short half slip

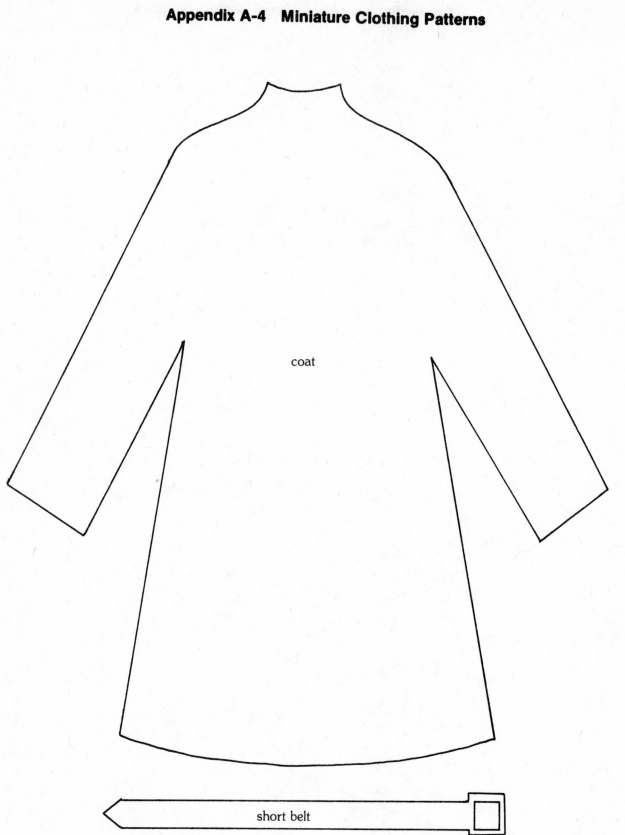

coat

short belt

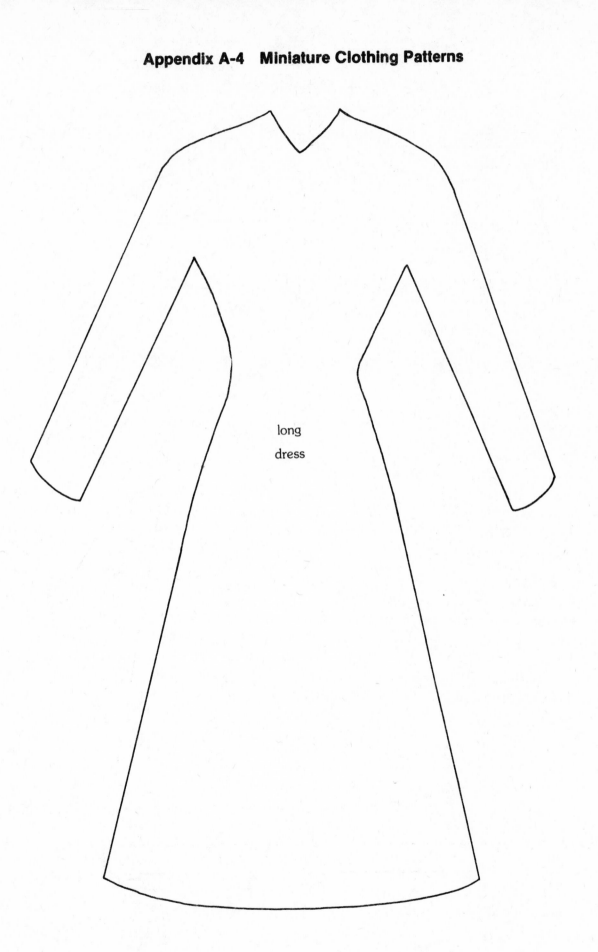

long

dress

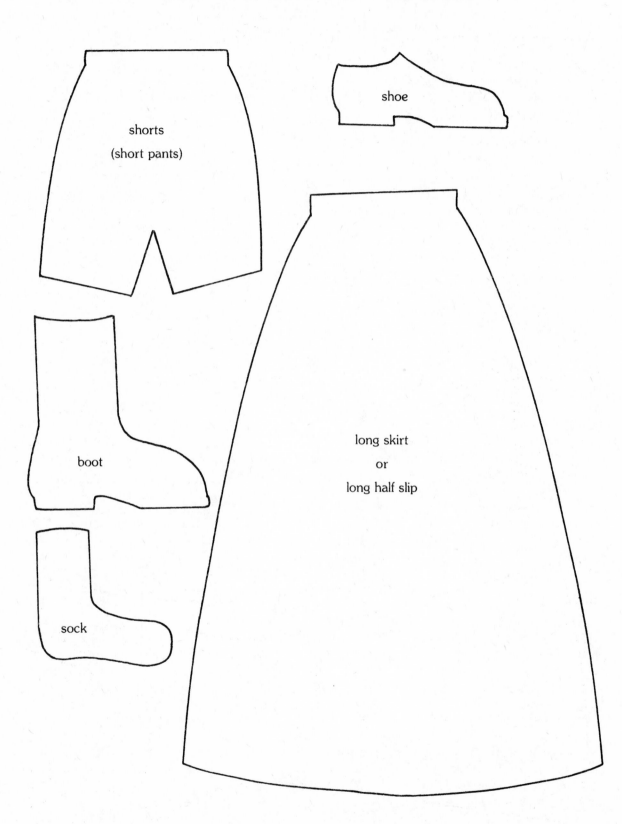

shorts

(short pants)

shoe

boot

sock

long skirt

or

long half slip

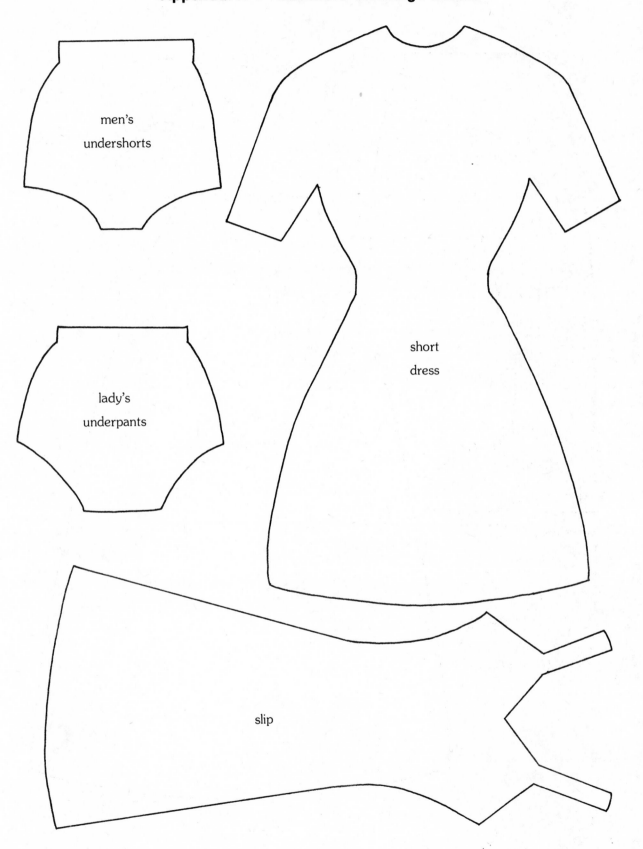

men's
undershorts

lady's
underpants

short

dress

slip

Appendix A-5   Deep or Shallow
Reproduce and mount pictures on twelve 3" x 4" cards to make object picture cards.

Appendix A-6 Flip Your Lid
Reproduce two sets of these pictures.
Glue one set of pictures inside box tops and the other set inside box bottoms.

Appendix A-6 Flip Your Lid
Reproduce and glue pictures to outside box tops.

Appendix A-6 Flip Your Lid
Reproduce and glue pictures to outside box bottoms.

Jane Smith
4321 First St.
Pleasant, Kansas
78194

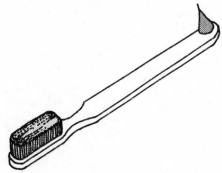

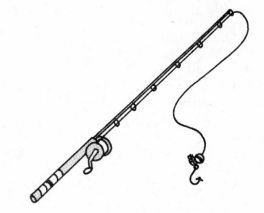

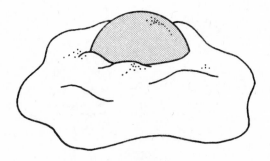

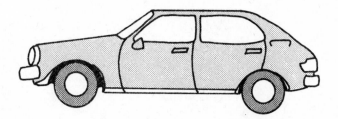

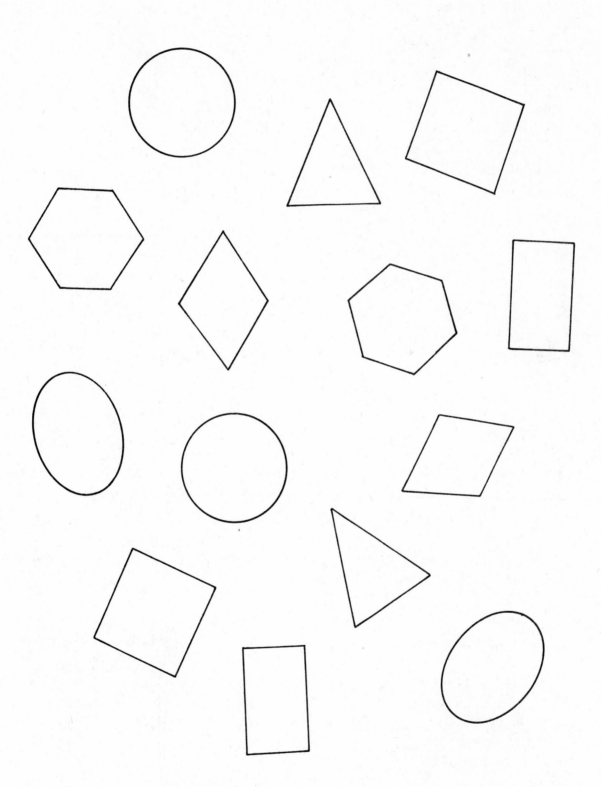

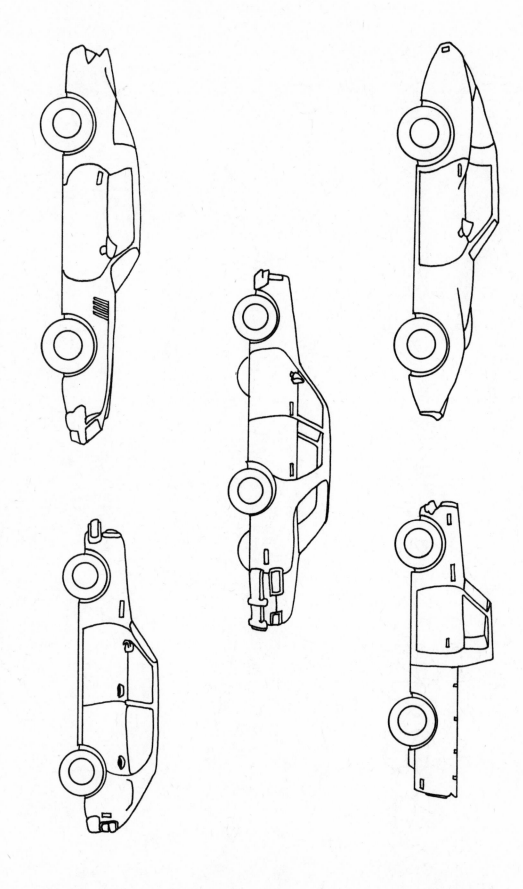

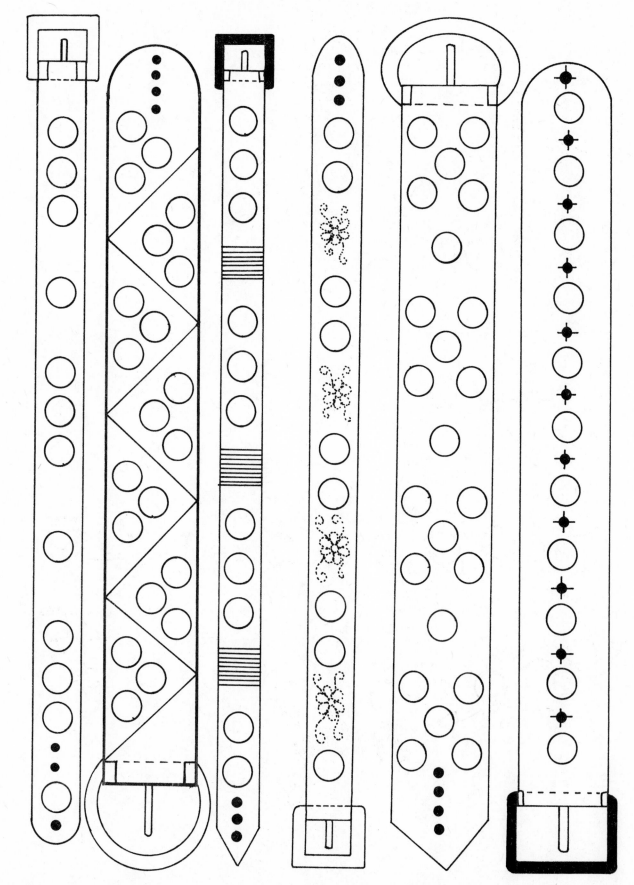

OPEN-ENDED SPINNER

1. Cut colored poster board square approximately 16" x 16".
2. Divide into six sections.
3. Cover with clear contact.
4. Cut arrow from a plastic bleach bottle, other plastic material, or poster board, and punch a hole.
5. In the center of the square, place a metal washer, then the arrow. (If a metal washer is not available, substitute a small poster board circle.)
6. Put a paper fastener through arrow, washer, and card. Bend back, leaving loose enough to spin.

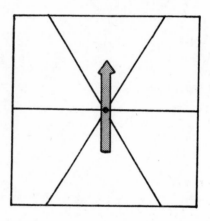

OPEN-ENDED TRAIL GAME BOARD

1. Use 22" x 28" white poster board.
2. Use marking pens to make a green START arrow, a red STOP sign, and black trails.

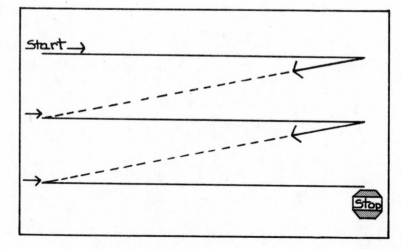

Appendix B
Instructions for Preparing Materials

EQUAL BOARDS

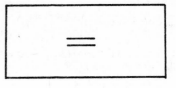

1. Cut 9″ x 12″ sheets of tagboard in half.
2. Put an equal sign (=) in the center of each piece.
3. Cover with clear contact.

BLINDFOLD

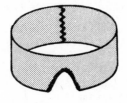

1. Buy a roll of Ace bandage 2½″ wide.
2. Cut a piece 20″ long.
3. Stitch ends together to form a band.
4. Clip in front to fit around a child's nose.
5. Overcast the nose cut.

GAME MARKERS

Suggestions for game markers:
- Aerosol spray can tops — names added with marking pen
- Large buttons — names on self-stick labels
- Empty thread spools — names on self-stick labels
- Poker chips — names added with marking pen
- Small blocks — names on self-stick labels

Appendix C Sources for Purchasing Materials

Charms and Novelties: U. S. Toy Company, Inc.
1040 East 85th
Kansas City, MO 64131

Coin Stamps: Innovative Educational Support Systems
P. O. Box 593
Wayne, NJ 07470

Developmental Learning Materials
7440 Natchez Avenue
Niles, IL 60648

DISCS (round clothespins): R. T. Duarte Company
South Merrimack, NH 03054

Picture Stickers: Word Making Productions, Inc.
P. O. Box 1858
Salt Lake City, UT 84110

Communication Skill Builders, Inc.
817 East Broadway
P. O. Box 6081-N
Tucson, AZ 85733

Thumbtack Puller: Chamro Company
717 Algonquin Avenue
Bensenville, IL 60106

Appendix D Index

Appendix D   Index (cont.)